Islam, Muslims and Media
Myths and Realities

Mohammad Ahmadullah Siddiqi

NAAMPS PUBLICATIONS
Chicago, London, Delhi

NAAMPS PUBLICATIONS
Chicago, London, Delhi

640 W. Irving Park Road
Chicago, IL 60613

Library of Congress Catalog Card Number: 97- 67121

ISBN 0-9641624-1-5

Cover Design: Abdul Malik Mujahid

Printed in the United States of America

Contents

Foreword

Communication and cultural relations are the necessary ingredients of Islamic community, or ummah. The Qur'an says: "We created you from a single(pair) of a male and a female, and made you into nations and tribes, that you may know each other (not so that you may despise each other). Verily the most honored of you in the sight of God is the one who (he/she) is the most righteous of you (Chapter 49: 13)." It is in this spiritual, political, social, and ethical framework that communications and understanding play a pervasive role in the preservation and maintenance of the unity of the Islamic community. Thus, communication on both interpersonal and social levels becomes basic as well as vital to the functioning of the community, for it sustains and encourages the integral and harmonious relations between God, the individual, and society.

The Islamic world consists of a vast and diverse geographical area stretching from Indonesia and the Pacific Ocean in the east to Morocco and the Atlantic coast in the west, from Central Asia and the Himalayas in the north to the southern African nations and the Indian Ocean. As one of the major religions in the world, Islam encompasses one quarter of the world's population -- over a billion people. From time of the Prophet Mohammed (A. D. 572 - 632) until the end of World War I and the demise of the Ottoman Empire, the Islamic community, consisting of various geographical units, was a major world power. With the rise of the modern nation-state system, coupled with the process of de-colonization and the birth of many new sovereign nations, the Islamic world politically, economically, and in some cases culturally, began to integrate into the existing sphere of the modern world system, with the West as a dominant actor. The contacts between the two cultures in the nineteenth and twentieth centuries and the absorption of many Islamic countries into quasi-secular political entities ranging from hereditary monarchies to modern western and/or military style republics created some of the most pronounced conflicts between the Islamic tradition and modern secularism.

Muslim Societies in general have a rather skeptical view of the West's information and media expansion, to say the least. The history of colonialism shows that the West extended its hold on Muslim heritage and resources not only economically and politically, but also culturally and through the expansion of their communication media and control of information. This colonial motivation developed in at least four distinct but interrelated stages, each reinforcing the others. In the first instance, missionaries, by establishing some of the first printing, publishing, and secular educational institutions in the Islamic world, laid the foundation not only for dissemination of religious ideas and values but also for the recruitment of a corps of educated elites who had to play a vital role in the process of political developments in later decades. This was followed in the second stage by the establishment of some of the early communications systems. This strategic use of information and image making helped to maintain European grip on power and gave economic and political advantage to complicit native leaders during the crises and anti-imperialist movements that swept Islamic lands in Asia and the Middle East in the nineteenth and early twentieth centuries. The rise of Orientalism and in classical Arabic and Persian orthography and bibliographical control of Islamic literature and arts was the third stage in the control and manipulation of information and images for strategic and political purposes. The fourth and current stage of information dissemination and control came about through the modern mass media, which were expanded globally by the West since World War II and became the major source of news and information about the Islamic lands. As the writings of the Orientalists and the West colored the images of Islam in the modern world and shaped the agenda of scientific inquiry and discourse, so did media affect the public perception of Islam.

In short, the history of colonialism and cultural imperialism of the last two centuries has shaped the perceptions of the Muslims in regard to the West and especially the United States. These perceptions are partly the result of the contradiction created between the words and the deeds of Europe and the United States, especially in relation to foreign affairs and cultural policies.

There is a misconception in the West and among the general public that Islam is only a religion. The division of the world into sacred and profane, religious and secular, and priesthood and laity does not exist in Islam. The separation of politics and ethics, and politics and economics, are all unnatural under the Islamic community paradigm. Islam is a total life system and, hence, the Islamic community provides guidance for the conduct of human activity. Race, ethnicity, tribalism, and nationalism have no place in distinguishing one member of the community from the rest. Nationalities, cultural differences, and geographical factors are recognized, but domination based on nationalism is rejected.

A number of studies on international communication over the last several decades reveal two essential characteristics: one is the ethnocentric orientation of the media systems in the highly industrialized nations, and the second is the "asymmetric" circulation of information in the world. The developments in the Islamic world not only have been reported during the period with a good deal of bias, distortion, and ethnocentrism by the Western media, but also the great portion of what has been reported has been provided mainly by the American and European media and journalists.

This is well illustrated by an example from the Persian Gulf War of 1990-1991. During that international conflict, journalists from the major Islamic countries opposing the intervention of the United States and the coalition forces not only were not allowed to be part of the news pool or to cover the countries involved in the war, but also the stream of information coming from the war front was controlled and manipulated either by governments involved or the Western news sources. A year later, genocide in Bosnia was not just being played out in the European theater: the stage and the audiences were much more complex, as millions of Muslims around the world watched the tragedy while the West did nothing. In an international system preoccupied with the nation state, Serbian leaders exploited the dominant vocabulary used by global media and political elites. A major psycho linguistic strategy was repeated in the media from the beginning. It referred to the Balkan conflict as a war between "Bosnian Serbs" and the "Bosnian Muslims." Notice that the natives, or the Bosnian Muslims, were introduced by their religious affiliation whereas the non-Muslim residents of Bosnia were described by their nationality and ethnic background as the "Bosnian Serbs" and not by their religion as Christians or members of the Orthodox church. And what about identifying Bosnian Muslims as Europeans? Are millions of Bosnian Muslims also Europeans or just remnants of the Ottoman Empire in Europe who are asking for an independent and unified Bosnia?

This book is not a mere academic exercise; it deals with practical issues and problems of the day. This volume represents a substantial step toward redressing a grave imbalance in the literature on Islam in the West at a moment in time when the need for it is great. Professor Mohammad A. Siddiqi's book, *Islam, Muslim, and the Media: Myths and Realities*, is an excellent addition to the critical examination of the role of the media in the coverage of Islam as well as a valuable source for an understanding of Islam and the Muslim community in America. Because the mass media set the agenda for the daily consideration of the issues by the public and because the media of all kinds are the sources of national and international images, it is necessary to understand how the media function if we wish to alter either the agenda or the structure of image-making processes in the United States.

There is furthermore a growing recognition that the concept of One World encompasses more than political and economic cooperation. It demands the conviction that in spite of the varieties of races, colors, faiths, and philosophies, there is unity in human suffering, dignity, and destiny. Islam has always known and practiced that principle. It is clear that cultural ecology and the organization and structure of international relations are at present in a period of profound change. The necessity of understanding and adaptation in our day and age seems ever more urgent and obvious than ever before.

Hamid Mowlana, Ph. D.
Professor of International Relations and Director,
International Communication Program,
American University, Washington, D. C.
President, International Association for Media and
Communication Research (IAMCR)

Introduction

Muslims in America are growing in Number as well as in their strength as a community. Their interaction and frustration with the media is also growing. They want themselves and their religion to be portrayed fairly and objectively. They complain about extreme media bias and deliberate distortions of their images.

Muslims, non-Muslims and the media ask questions such as: Do the media deliberately distort the images of Muslims and Islam? Are they (the media) presenting Islam as the eminent threat in the post Cold War era? Why is there so much Muslim and Islam bashing in the media? Are most Muslims fundamentalists by the very nature of their religion? Does Islam preach violence against those who do not adhere to its teachings? Does Islam treat women as inferior to men? Do Muslims in the U. S. support terrorists in the Middle East and elsewhere?

Unfortunately, these and similar questions have not been answered to the satisfaction of anyone. Muslims see media as the greatest conspirator against them and Islam. The media examine Muslims within their own perspectives -- secular/ Christian/capitalist. Often these perspectives lack facts, accuracy and the right context.

This book provides a more realistic understanding of the Muslims' concern about their portrayal in the media. It provides answers, to both Muslims and the general readers, to questions such as the above.

To Muslims, the book offers suggestions, in Chapter Six, for establishing mutually beneficial media relations, focusing on media's role as an effective channel for reaching out to Americans at large.

For media, this can be used as a resource book for writing about Islam and Muslims in America. It gives the media practitioner a Muslim perspective (an insider's view) of Islam and the Muslim community in America, its concerns, and the issues that confront it as one of the fastest growing communities in this country. A glossary of Islamic terms is provided at the end of Chapter Four. This may serve as a style book for media practitioners when writing or broadcasting about Islam and Muslims.

For general American readers, the book offers an understanding of Islam and the Muslim community in America.

For professionals and academics, this study serves as a basis for further research and study into the portrayal of religion in popular American media. The book may also be used in classes of multi-culturism and diversity, sociology, communication, and international studies as a supplementary textbook to provide students with a picture of Islam, Muslims, and the diversity that exists within Islam and among Muslims.

I am greatly indebted to many colleagues, both in the Muslim community and outside, who provided their valuable suggestions to make this book more relevant to the readers. Special thanks are due to Aslam Abdullah, Shahid Athar, Laurent Bryant, Waris Cowlas, Yvonne Haddad, Andrew Hermann, Asad Husain, Fayyaz Khan, Aminah McCloud, Hamid Mowlana, Abdul Malik Mujahid, Nejatullah Siddiqi, and Michael Suleiman who encouraged me at every step of this project by their critiques, suggestions, and comments. Thanks are also due to my two cousins, Arshad and Khalid, for keeping up the vigil to publish the book. I am also thankful to my colleague Jim Courter for editing suggestions. And finally, many thanks to my wife Tayyeba and children Shazia and Kamran for their strong support and encouragement, and for giving up their time with me for completing the manuscript.

Mohammad Ahmadullah Siddiqi
Western Illinois University

CHAPTER ONE

Historical Overview

Images are very important to a civilization, culture and religion because as humans people wish to have a good image. There is nothing essentially good or bad in images themselves, but only in what they portray, evoke or justify. Image, as Fox (1994) describes, refers to "any form of mental, pictorial representation, however generic or fleeting." For most people, in most cultures, the major source of information about other people, cultures and religions is the media; we believe what we read, especially what we see. This is particularly true of television.

"Television," as Costanzo (1994) observes, "will continue to shape our culture and our institutions. Its appeal to community and its influence on how we read images will continue to be major factors in our national life." The new information technologies are capable of creating instant history and provide live images from distant locations to our living rooms.

Desert Storm, the Persian Gulf War, was an unprecedented event reflecting the triumph of orchestrated imagery by the media. As Gerbner (1994) observes, "image-driven and violence-laden, compelling as it is contrived, instant history robs us of reflection time, critical distance, political space, and access to alternatives." So when on October 3, 1994, the "Eye on America" segment of the CBS Evening News broadcasted a program holding American Muslim organizations and mosques responsible for funding terrorist activities in the Middle East, instantly the Ikhwa mosque in New York City and the Islamic Center in Yuba City, California were firebombed and properties worth millions of dollars were destroyed. American Muslims were shocked. How could they and their religion be perceived as violent?

It is important to study this subject in detail and analyze as well as understand the nature of media coverage of Islam and Muslims.

The historical overview presented in this chapter traces the nature, extent, and the roots of the media's portrayal of Muslims and Islam as it has been examined in previous studies. This will foster better understanding of the current situation and also help analyze the themes and the contents of present-day media portrayal of Muslims and Islam.

Historians, sociologists and anthropologists, among others, have been challenged for centuries in their attempts to classify and define different civilizations and cultures. Spengler (1926), Berdyaev (1936), Northrop (1946), Sorokin (1950), Cowell (1952), Malinowski (1955), Daniel (1975), and Huntington (1993, 1996), among others, have attempted to classify and define cultures and civilizations. Some of these scholars have been very optimistic in their analyses. Analyzing Huntington's thesis, Braibanti (1995) states that "Northrop emphasizes the mutuability of cultures and attempts to discover the ideological bases for their compatibility. He classifies cultures into two broad categories: East and West. 'It should be eventually possible,' he concludes, 'to achieve a society for mankind generally in which the higher standard of living of the most scientifically advanced and theoretically guided Western nations is combined with the compassion, the universal sensitivity to the beautiful, and the abiding equanimity and calm joy of the spirit which characterizes the sages and many of the humblest people of the orient.' "

Huntington, however, sees Islam as the most probable enemy of the West. In his article, "The Clash of Civilization," which appeared in 1993 issue of *Foreign Affairs*, Huntington warns that Islam poses the most serious security threat for the West. It is between these two extreme contexts -- the highly optimistic and mostly pessimistic -- that most studies have examined the portrayal of Islam and Muslims in the media.

Before the Iranian revolution in 1979, most of the media portrayal of Muslims and Islam was limited to Arab images in the media. In one of the earliest studies of Middle East news in American media, Sulieman (1965) found that Arabs were portrayed in American newsmagazines as backward and nomads. "Fairness is sacrificed," notes Jack Shaheen (1984), "when producers and writers go into a series with preconceived ideas about people. As we know, notorious Arabs do not appear in a single series, but they are scattered among numerous programs." After analyzing numerous television documentaries portraying stereotypical images of Arabs, Shaheen concludes, "when one ethnic or minority group is degraded, for whatever reason, we all (Americans) suffer." As for the Arab images, he wonders, "how would Jewish-Americans react if they witnessed a host of TV shylocks posing as nuclear terrorists? Would the blacks welcome being portrayed as white-slavers? Would Hispanics be chagrined if they were shown, along with Orientals, as crude foreigners buying up America?" Shaheen (1990) further notes that most often Westerners have tried to understand the Image of Islam through a distorted picture of the Arab nations and that Western media have played a significant role in this distortion. In a recent article, analyzing the 1995 Disney movie "Father of the Bride II," Shaheen (1996) notes, "The prejudice in Disney's Bride II and other films engender among America's Muslims and Arabs feelings of insecurity, vulnerability, alienation and even denial of heritage."

Many recent studies have analyzed the movies and television documentaries' portrayal of Muslims and Islam in general. The images presented in these have been much more dramatic, powerful and negative. The *Sheikh* (1921), *Lawrence of Arabia* (1962), *Black Sunday* (1977), *The Formula* (1980), *Rollover* (1981), *Jewel of the Nile* (1985), and *Delta Force* (1986) are among such movies and television documentaries portraying a negative and violent image of Muslims.

After conducting a qualitative and quantitative analysis of two major movies -- *Lawrence of Arabia* and *The Message* -- depicting Muslim and Arab culture and civilization, Rehman (1992 (a) concludes that "Hollywood, with few exceptions, has viewed the Muslim world as an exotic, strange, and violent place." He notes that the film directors and writers rely on negative stereotypes and inflame international misunderstanding and unrest. Most such movies, according to Rehman, are successful in creating myths such as 1) all Muslims are Arabs and all Arabs are

Muslims; 2) the Arab families are self destructive; and 3) all Palestinians are terrorists. In another study Rehman (1992 (b) has analyzed two other movies, *Cannonball Run* (1979) and *Protocol* (1983). He observes that the portrayal of Arabs and Muslims is too offending and negative.

Al-Zahrani (1988), in his study of the US television and press coverage of Islam and Muslims, suggests that the television news in general report Arab and Muslim issues mostly in a negative manner, lacking balance and objectivity. Most other studies of television coverage of Muslims and Islam -- Adams (1981); Altheide (1976); Asi (1981); Atwater (1986); Ghareeb (1983); Heumann (1980); Kern (1981); Paraschos (1985); Said (1981); and Woll (1987) -- have also concluded that the portrayal lacks objectivity and fairness.

Print media have been studied more extensively, for they provide more Muslim and Islamic images on a daily basis. Studies of the print media suggest that the print media portrayal of Islam and Muslims is even more distorted. Shaheen (1985) notes that the American press presents Islam and Muslims negatively, and as terrorists. A common trend among American reporters is to stereotype the act of an individual or a group as being representative of the entire Muslim community or Islam. This seldom happens in the case of other groups such as Christians, Jews, Blacks, or Hispanics. Allen (1990) agrees with this observation of taking stereotypes a step further to place all people of one color, race, or origin in one category and treat them as a homogeneous group. Said (1981 and 1987), in his studies of the Western and American media and Islam, suggests that the media portray Islam and Muslims as being responsible for all the ills of this century everywhere in the world. Gahreeb (1984) notes that even prestigious newspapers such as the *Washington Post* portray Muslims as terrorist. Oxtoby (1980) finds Arabs being depicted as religious fanatics whose religion embraces such concepts as "assassin" and "jihad." While analyzing the media coverage of the Middle East, Said (1987) notes the presence of six major themes:

1) Arab or Islamic terrorism and Arab or Islamic terrorists states or groups;
2) Revival of Islamic movements and the Muslim awakening associated with a phrase, "the return of Islam";
3) The Middle East as the origin of violence and terrorism;
4)The Middle East as backward, excepting Israel and sometimes Turkey;
5) The Middle East as a place for the re-emergence of so-called anti-semitism;
6) The Middle East as the home of the PLO.

Another recurring theme, according to Mughees-uddin (1993), that has become more popular in recent times, is that of the so-called "Islamic Fundamentalism," and its link to violence and terrorism. "Islam," according to Mughees-uddin "will be the next threat candidate for the U. S. media after the end of the Cold War." Afzal (1991) notes that the American media portray Muslims and Islam as anti-modern, anti-progress, uncivil and anti-West. He argues that the media portrayal is designed to dehumanize the Arabs and Muslims so that their destruction can be made palatable. In a more recent study, Afzal (1993) suggests that the main focus of media in the remaining years of this century will be on the so-called "Islamic terrorism" which has become almost synonymous to "Islamic fundamentalism." Zaidi (1991), in an article titled "Medium is the Mischief," presents two cases, one representing a series of articles in *The New York Times* and the other in the *Washington Post*. He points to the extreme bias of these two newspapers as they present a very distorted image of his home country, Pakistan. *The Message International*, a Muslim magazine published by a New York-based Muslim organization, compares the overall treatment of Muslims by the mass Media to that of mental tyranny. A number of studies -- Ali (1984); Al-Marayati (1994); Brewda (1990); Badran (1985); Belkaoui (1978); Dart and Allen (1994); Gerbner (1984); Ghandour (1985); Haynes (1983); Mortimer (1981); Mousa (1984); Mughees--uddin (1992); Parenti (1986); Sheler (1990); Terry (1974); and Wagner (1973) -- have also looked into the portrayal of Arabs, Muslims, and Islam in the US. print media, and have arrived at conclusions similar to those discussed above. In Suleiman's (1993) words, "The term Arab, Arabism, Arab nationalism, and the religion associated with them, i.e., Islam (and Muslims), have been given an extremely negative connotation in the United States."

Many scholars have traced the roots of the conflict between Islam and the West. Esposito (1992) observes that, "despite common theological roots and centuries-long interaction, Islam's relationship to the West has often been marked by mutual ignorance, stereotyping, contempt, and conflict."

Islam's early history of expansions and victories has always posed a challenge to the followers of other faiths. In recent times the Iranian revolution in 1979, the resurgence of Islam throughout Muslim and non Muslim countries, and the situation in the Middle East have inculcated a sense of fear and antagonism among many of the non-Muslim historians, theologians, politicians and policy makers. Amos Perlmutter (1993) reflects this fear and antagonism by warning about "a general Islamic war waged against the West, Christianity, modern capitalism, Zionism and communism all at once." He argues that an all-out "war against Muslim populism" should be the top priority of the West.

Professor Bernard Lewis (1990), in his Thomas Jefferson Memorial lecture, which was later published in the *Atlantic Monthly* under the title, "The Roots of Muslim Rage, " tries to isolate Islam by presenting it as a threat to the "Judeo-Christian heritage." The provocative term "rage" had earlier been used by the *Los Angeles Times* journalist, Robin Wright (1979) in her book, *Sacred Rage: The Wrath of Militant Islam.* Bernard Lewis considers the resurgence of Islam as "no less than a clash of civilizations." He sees Islam as "an ancient rival against our Judeo-Christian heritage, our present and our world-wide expansion of both." Lewis, a renowned historian and scholar, demonstrates the same secular bias that has become a part of the media culture. However, both the media and scholars ignore that part of the history which is filled with stark confrontation between Judaism and Christianity and cooperation and co-existence among Jews, Christians and Muslims.

When Muslims liberated Jerusalem in 638 CE, Christian churches and shrines in that area became the popular sites of pilgrimage for Christians from all over the World. Jews, who were banned from living in Jerusalem by the Christian rulers, were permitted to return. Muslims built a shrine, the Dome of the Rock, and a mosque, the Al-Aqsa, near the Wailing Wall, one of the most significant Jewish sites, thus establishing the most significant Judo-Christian-Islamic heritage in Jerusalem. From that time until the beginning of the Crusades in the 11th century, Muslims, Christians and Jews enjoyed five centuries of peaceful co-existence. Unfortunately, the terms Crusades and Jihad (the holy war), have been widely misunderstood by many Christians, Jews and Muslims.

The legacy of the Crusades, as well as that of the Muslim Jihad, depends upon where one stands in history. The history that is taught in American grade schools focuses more on confrontations and differences among Muslims,

Christians and Jews than on cooperation and similarities. More sadly, some of this history is distorted to the disadvantage of Muslims. For example, there is hardly any mention of the thousands and thousands of Jews who have been massacred during the Crusades, whereas the confrontation and war between Muslims and Christians and the conflicts between Muslims and Jews have been enlarged greatly out of proportion. Most of us do not know that during the Crusades, while Christians were fighting Muslims, they learned a great deal from them in Mathematics, Astronomy, Chemistry and Medicine. "At a time when few Europeans could read or write, " notes Wormser (1994), "there were 400,000 manuscripts in the library of Cordoba, Spain, alone." Many European scholars traveled to the universities in Muslim Spain, Damascus in Syria, Cairo in Egypt, and Baghdad and Basra in Iraq to copy the latest medical, mathematical, and philosophical manuscripts that were later translated into Latin. Our images of Muslims and Islam would be different if we knew that Muslims, Christians and Jews share much in their monotheistic traditions, and the much- talked-about Judeo-Christian heritage is in fact a Judo-Christian-Islamic heritage. Islam is the last and the latest of the three faiths. Qur'an, the source book of Islam, clearly states the relationship between all divine faiths:

> Lo! We inspired you (Muhammad) as We inspired Noah and the prophets after him, as We inspired Abraham and Ishmael and Isaac and Jacob and the tribes, and Jesus and Job and Jonah and Aaron and Solomon, and as We imparted unto David and Psalms (Qur'an: 4-163)

It is important to our understanding of the world's religions that we know the fact that Judaism, Christianity and Islam have all been inspired by the same God. A better and correct understanding of the people of other faiths will help reduce the gap that currently exists between them. It is unfortunate that the media focuses more on highlighting the tensions and conflicts among people than the roots of understanding and cooperation that is at the core of people's survival as human beings.

Historically, as notes Montagu (1968), "throughout the two million years of man's evolution the highest premium has been placed on cooperation, not merely intragroup cooperation, but also inter-group cooperation, or else there would be no human beings today." One of the main focuses of Islam is its emphasis on one universal human nation (Qur'an: 2-213). Qur'an and numerous sayings of Muhammad describe the killing of a single human being without a valid reason as killing of the entire human race. In contrast, the contemporary corporate culture survives by dividing people and by antagonizing them. That is why most Americans are led to perceive Muslims as the "others" in relation to the "we'" or "us," the Americans. It then becomes easier to direct our hostility towards those others who are not from among us. Although talking about pluralism and diversity has become the norm, polarization in society appears to be increasing. Media undoubtedly play a pivotal role in this polarization. Gerbner (1995) rightly points out ". . . the word media has lost its meaning of plurality. Media coalesce into a seamless, pervasive, and increasingly homogenized cultural environment that has drifted out of democratic reach." The next two chapters illustrate this point with examples from the media as they treat Islam and Muslims.

References

Adams, W. C. (1981). *Television Coverage of the Middle East*. Norwood, NJ.: Ablex.

Afzal, Omar (1991, January). The American Media's Middle East War. *The Message International*: 19-20.

__________ (1993, March). Media's new Shooting Targets. *The Message ,International*: 17-18.

Al-Marayati, Salam (1994, June). The Rising Tide of Hostile Stereotyping of Islam. *The Washington Report on Middle East Affairs*: 27.

Al-Zahrani, Abdul Aziz A. (1988). U. S. Television and Press Coverage of Islam and Muslims. Doctoral dissertation, Norman, Oklahoma: University of Oklahoma.

Ali, M. (1984). Western Media and the Muslim World. *The Concept,* v. 4 (2): 13-19.

Allen, Irving Lewis (1990). *Unkind Words: Ethnic Labeling from Red skins to WASP.* New York: Bergin & Garvey.

Altheide, D (1976). *Creating Reality: How TV News Distorts Events.* Beverly Hills, CA: Sage.

Asi, M. O. (1981). Arabs, Israelis and U. S. Television Networks: A Content Analysis of How ABC, CBS, and NBC Reported the News Between 1970 - 1979. Doctoral dissertation, Ohio University. *Dissertation Abstract International,* v. 42: 893A.

Atwater , T. (1986, August). Terrorism on the Evening News: An Analysis of Coverage of the TWA Hostage Crisis on "NBC Nightly News." Paper presented to the Radio-Television Journalism Division, AEJMC 1986 Convention, Norman, Oklahoma.

Badran, A. B. (1985). Editorial Treatment of the Arab-Israeli Conflict in U. S. and European Newspapers: 1980 - 1982. Doctoral dissertation, University of Massachusetts. *Dissertation Abstract International*, v. 45: 3021A.

Belkaoui, J. M. (1978). Images of Arabs and Israelis in the Prestige Press: 1966 - 1974. *Journalism Quarterly*, v. 55: 732-733 & 799.

Berdyaev, Nicholas (1936). *The Meaning of History.* London: The Centenary Press, 1936: 207-224.

Braibanti, Ralph (1995). *The Nature and Structure of the Islamic World.* Chicago: International Policy and Strategy Institute: 16-22, 90.

Brewada, Joseph (1990, July 20). Super Powers Prepare Middle East War: Final Solution to Arab Problems. *Executive Intelligence Review*: 28-30.

Costanzo, William V. (1994). Reading Ollie North, in Roy F. Fox (ed.), *Images in Language, Media, and Mind.* Urbana, Illinois: National Council of Teachers of English: 108-122.

Cowell, F. R. (1952). *History, Civilization and Culture.* Boston: Beacon Press: 9.

Daniel, Norman (1975). *The Cultural Barrier: Problems in the Exchange of Ideas.* Edinburgh: Edinburgh University Press: 13-14.

Dart, John and Jimmy Allen (1994). *Bridging the Gap: Religion and the News Media.* Nashville: The Freedom Forum First Amendment Center at Vanderbilt University.

Esposito, John L. (1992). *The Islamic Threat: Myth or Reality*? New York: Oxford University Press.

Fox, Roy F. (ed. 1994). *Images in Language, Media, and Mind.* Urbana, Illinois: National Council of Teachers of English: x.

Gerbner, G. (1995). Forward: What's Wrong With This Picture, in Kamalipour, Yahya R. (ed.) *The U. S. Media and the Middle East: Image and Perception.* Westport, Connecticut: Greenwood Press: xv.

___________ (1994). Instant History: Lessons from the Persian Gulf War, in Roy F. Fox (ed.), op. cit.: 123-140.

Gerbner, G. and Marvanx G. (1984). The Many Worlds of the World's Press, in G. Gerbner & M. Siefert (eds.) *World Communication: A Handbook.* New York: Longman: 92-102.

Ghandour, N. H. (1985). Coverage of the Arab World and Israel in American News Magazines Between 1975 and 1981: A Comparative Content Analysis. Doctoral dissertation, Teachers College of Columbia University. *Dissertation Abstract International,* v. 45: 2476A.

Ghareeb, E. (1984). The Middle East in the U. S. Media. *The Middle East Annual Issues and Events*, v. 3: 185- 210.

__________ (1983). A Renewed Look at the American Coverage of the Arabs: Toward a Better Understanding, in E. Ghareeb (ed.) *Split Vision, the Portrayal of Arabs in the American Media*. Washington, D. C.: American Arab Affairs Council: 157-194.

Haynes, J. E. (1983). Keeping Cool about Kabul: *The Washington Post* and *The New York Times* Cover the Communist Seizure of Afghanistan. *World Affairs*, v. 145: 369-383.

Heumann, J. (1980). U. S. Network Television: Melodrama and the Iranian Crisis. *Middle East Review*, v. 13: 51-55.

Huntington, Samuel P. (1996). *The Clash of Civilization and the Remaking of World Order*. New York: Simon and Schuster.

__________(1993). The Clash of Civilization? , *Foreign Affairs*, v. 72, #3: 22-49.

Kern, M. (1981). The Invasion of Afghanistan: Domestic Vs. Foreign Stories, in W. C. Adams (ed.), op. cit.: 106-127.

Lewis, Bernard (1990, September). The Roots of Muslim Rage. *The Atlantic Monthly*: 47-60.

Malinowski, Bronislaw (1955). *The Dynamics of Culture Change*. New Haven: Yale University Press: 17-40.

Montagu, Ashley (ed., 1968). *Man and Aggression*. London: Oxford University Press: 34.

Mortimer, E. (1981). Islam and the Western Journalist. *Middle East Journal*, v. 35: 492-505.

Mousa, I. S. (1984). *The Arab Images in the U. S. Press*. New York: Peter Lang.

Mughees-uddin (1993). Many Voices One Chorus: Framing Islam and Islamic Movements (FIS and Hamas) in the US Elite Press (*The New York Times*, the *Washington Post* and the *Los Angeles Times*). Paper presented at the First Conference of the North American Association of Muslim Professionals and Scholars, Chicago, April 9-11.

__________(1992). Editorial Treatment of U. S. Foreign Policy in *The New York Times*: The Case of Pakistan (1980-90). Paper presented to the

International Communication Division of the AEJMC Convention, Montreal, Canada, August 7.

Northrop, F. S. C. (1946). *The Meeting of East and West.* New York: Macmillan: 296.

Oxtoby, W. G. (1980). Western Perception of Islam and the Arabs, in M. C. Hudson & R. G. Wolf (eds.) *The American Media and the Arabs.* Washington, D. C. : Georgetown University Press: 3-12.

Paraschos, M. Rutherford B. (1985). Network News Coverage of Invasion of Lebanon by Israel in 1982. *Journalism Quarterly*, v. 62: 457-464.

Parenti, M. (1986). *Inventing Reality: The Politics of Mass Media.* New York: St. Martin's Press.

Perlmutter, Amos (1993, January 22). Islamic Fundamentalist Network. *The Washington Times.*

Rehman, Sharaf N. (1992.a, January/February). Muslim Images in American Cinema. *The Minaret*: 39-42.

________________(1992.b). Portrayal of the Arabs in the Western Mass Media (pp. 153-162), in Dilnawaz A. Siddiqui and Abbas F. Allkhafaji. *The Gulf War: Implications for the Global Business and Media.* Apollo, Pennsylvania: Closson Press.

Said E. W. (1981). *Covering Islam: How the Media and the Experts Determine How We See Rest of the World.* New York: Pantheon Books.

__________(1987). The MESA Debate: The Scholars, the Media and the Middle East. *Journal of Palestine Studies*, v. 16 (2): 85-104.

Shaheen, J. G. (1984). *The TV Arab.* Bowling Green, Ohio: Bowling Green State University Popular Press.

_____________ (1985, November), Media Coverage of the Middle East: Perception and Foreign Policy. *Annals*, v. 482: 160-174.

_____________ (1990, August 25). Our Cultural Demon: The Ugly Arab. *Des Moines Register*: 7 A.

_____________ (1996, March/April). Disney Has Done It Again. *Islamic Horizon*: 38-39.

Sheler, Jeffery L. (1990, August 8). Islam in America. *U. S. News & World Report*: 69-71.

Sorokin, Pitirim A. (1950). *Social Philosophies in an Age of Crisis*. Boston: Beacon Press: 279.

Spengler, Oswald (1926). *The Decline of the West*. New York: Alfred Knopf, v. 1: 32.

Suleiman, M. W. (1965). An Evaluation of the Middle East News Coverage in Seven American News Magazines, July- December , 1965. *Middle East Forum*, v. 41: 9-30.

________________ (1993). American Views of Arabs and the Impact of These Views on Arabs in the United States, paper presented at the Arab Sociological Association Conference, 29 March - 1 April: 6.

Terry, J. & Mendenhall, G. (1974). 1973 U. S. Press Coverage on Middle East. *Journal of Palestine Studies*, v. 4 (1): 120-133.

Wagner, C. H. (1973). Elite American Newspapers Opinion and the Middle East: Commitment Versus Isolation, in W. A. Beling (ed.) *The East: Quest for American Policy*. Albany: State University of New York Press: 306-335.

Woll, Allen L. & Randell M. Miller (1987). *Ethnic and Racial Images in American Television*. New York: Garland Publishing.

Wormser, Richard (1994). *American Islam*. New York: Walker and Company: 10.

Wright, Robin (1979). *Sacred Rage: The Wrath of Militant Islam*. New York: Linden Press.

Zaidi, Nayyar (1991, January). Medium is the Mischief. *The Message International*: 25-26.

CHAPTER TWO

Islam and Media

> One of the strangest facts in today's world is that Islam, a religion which in many ways is almost identical with Christianity and Judaism, should be so poorly understood in Europe and America (James A. Michener, 1955).

Michener wrote the above in *Reader's Digest* forty three years ago, but the situation is not any better today. Islam still is one of the most misunderstood religions in the world. A large number of the so-called experts on Islam, the Middle East and terrorism give the impression that their interpretation of Islamic beliefs, practices and events is fair, balanced and responsible. However, what the consumers of news get from these experts is a distorted and inflated image of Islam. Islam appears to be a racially biased and culturally uncivilized religion, perpetuating violence and hatred against people of other faiths. Often Islam is lumped with underdevelopment, thereby creating a feeling of economic insecurity among people and forcing them to remain at a distance from Islam. As the following examples suggest, the media continuously remind the American people about the dangers and ills of Islam, sometimes in a threatening way, and at other times in a subtle way, creating myths and stereotypes.

> Islam is a communal way of life and the vast majority of emigrants and their European-born children live together isolated from, and hostile to, the society around them...The Muslim communities demand to be allowed to retain all aspects of Islam, including laws unacceptable to the West (such as blood vengeance and killing of females for [sic] in revenge for the desecration of family honor, to name but a few), and argue for making Islamic law superior to the civil law of the land (Pipes, 1992).

The quote above is a good example of making erroneous association between "blood vengeance and the killing of females" with Islam. The author relies on isolated incidents of male members of a family attacking daughters or siblings based on personal indignation and not on a community's desire to implement Islamic law. The attack on the Muslims living in Europe indicates that they are dormant militants awaiting the order from extremists to incite violence. In a cartoon, appearing in the *Chicago Tribune*, the caption is titled, "Violence the Islamic Curse." In the article associated with the cartoon, Professor Raphael Patai implicates Islam with violence:

> In the West, assassination has become typically a political act, while in the Moslem world it was, and remained, primarily a religious deed.

Violence, the Islamic curse

The claim that assassination is primarily a religious deed is totally unfounded in Qur'an and other sources of Islamic knowledge. One neither finds the same treatment given to violent acts committed by the followers of other faiths, nor are the Christian or Judaic ethics blamed for a violent act committed by a follower of either of these religions. The purpose of this discourse is neither to defend Islam nor to condone violence in Islamic societies, but to describe the uses of Islam by the media and, to a certain extent, provide accurate information from the direct sources of Islamic knowledge such as the Qur'an.

Islamic fundamentalism has been a major concern to many among the media scholars and experts. It is viewed as a major threat to the West. It is often associated with any form of Islamic resistance against the existing dictatorial and unrepresentative governments in the Middle East. It is considered to be a force that is out to destroy any modern culture and civilization. It is proven to be against the Judeo-Christian heritage. It is presented as a violent, radical and extreme form of Islamic behavior. The following examples are but a small sample of such representation of Islam by the media:

> If communism has often been described as a disease, Islamic fundamentalism is a plague now infecting the entire Islamic world from Morocco to India... [It is] a very real representation of the anti-Western , anti-modern forces in the Arab and Islamic World (Perlmutter, 1993).

> Ultimately, the struggle of the fundamentalists is against two enemies, secularism and modernism... This is no less than a clash of civilizations--the perhaps irrational but surely historic reaction of an ancient rival against our Judeo-Christian heritage, our secular present and our world wide expansion of both (Lewis, 1990).

> This generation of Islamic fundamentalists have embraced the concept of "jihad" or struggle and emphasized its meaning as violent warfare. (Steinfles, 1993).

> This is the dark side of Islam, which shows its face in violence and terrorism intended to overthrow modernizing, more secular regimes and harm the Western nations that support them (Nelan, 1993).

In order to understand the inaccuracies of the above assertions and the extent of misrepresentation of Islam, it is important to understand the meaning of the central term that has been used in the above examples. Fundamentalists have been traditionally meant to be those Christians, especially the Protestant Christians, who believed that the Bible should be followed literally. This definition is applied to all Muslims, practicing or non-practicing, because Qur'an is viewed by all Muslims as the literal word of God. The Qur'an's purity and the divine nature of its text has never been an issue among Muslims, Sunnis and Shias alike. No theological doctrine separates the fundamentalists from the non-fundamentalists. Most media practitioners do not understand this context and indiscriminately use the term "Islamic fundamentalism," which was coined as the aftermath of the Iranian revolution in 1979. Anytime a Muslim group tries to organize itself to undo the injustices done to them, they are quickly branded as "Islamic fundamentalists."

For the last several centuries Muslims were exploited by the colonial powers of the West, and after the Second World War they have been facing the tyranny and oppression of their self-imposed rulers. Most of these Muslims, even most of those living in the oil-rich Persian Gulf countries, are poor and illiterate. They have no say in the political process and economic affairs of their countries. Their search for justice, equality, democracy and human rights has been going on for about half a century, yet most of them are subjected to inhuman treatment by their own governments. In such circumstances, when a group of Muslims tries to experiment with Islam's political, social and economic systems, they are labeled as fundamentalists. Even in cases where Islamic groups are elected through a fair and democratic process, such as in the North-African nation of Algeria, the media portrays them as fundamentalists, while the takeover by the military junta is presented as a better alternative.

Yossef Bodansky and Forrest Vaughn (1990 and 1992) authored several reports on behalf of the House Republican's Task Force on Terrorism and Unconventional Warfare. In these reports they purportedly uncover a global conspiracy by Muslim fundamentalists to incite violence and terrorism in order to weaken or eliminate the Western powers. According to this report, Muslim fundamentalists are devious, self-centered, power-hungry, and war mongers. Although the authors provide "facts," there is no attribution, and no one can verify the accusations. Over the past several years, a number of publications have published special reports and columns implicating Islam as the most significant threat to the liberal democracies of the West. These include, among others, *Time* (1993), *The Economist* (1992), *The New York Times* (1993), *U. S. News & World Report* (1993), and *Chicago Tribune* (1995). Some of these reports are so inflammatory that if taken seriously, they will lead to a great misunderstanding between Muslims and other people in Western societies. For example, Mortimer B. Zuckerman, editor-in-chief of *U. S. News & World Report* and publisher of the *Atlantic Monthly* writes:

> Islam's militant strain is on the verge of replacing communism as the principal opponent of Western liberal democracy and the values it enshrines . . . The Gulf War was just one paragraph in the long conflict between the West and radical Islam; the World Trade Center bombing , just a sentence. We are in for a long struggle not amenable to reasoned dialogue (Zuckerman, 1993).

It is difficult to substantiate Zuckerman's promise of a dreadful outcome in case Islamic groups prevail in Muslim countries. While most Muslim governments have failed to deal with social problems such as poverty, hunger, illiteracy, and homelessness, Islamic activists in Algeria, Egypt, Jordan, Pakistan, Sudan, and many other Muslim countries have been successfully conducting social and welfare programs on a mass scale with considerable success over the last several decades. This can be confirmed by many regional agencies' reports, local media coverage of such events and the various annual reports of the United Nations and UNESCO.

In a recent Jewish-Muslim convention, held in Glenco, Illinois (a Chicago suburb), many of the Rabbis who recently visited Israel, the West Bank and Ghaza confirmed that even in those areas most successful programs are conducted by members of the Islamic groups, including Hamas. These programs include conducting large-scale relief operations to feed the hungry and help the needy, operating hospitals and schools, and even managing small-scale banks and financial institutions. It is because of their momentous work to benefit people that Islamists enjoy grass-root support, and not because of their or Islam's radicalism.

It is indeed very important for us to understand the nature of unrest that leads to violence and indiscriminate acts of terrorism by certain Muslims, both individuals and groups. These acts of terrorism have always been unconditionally condemned by Muslims in the United States. Immediately after the World Trade Center bombing, Muslim leaders and organizations from all across America convened press conferences in New York, Los Angeles, and Washington, D. C., and issued a strong statement condemning the terrorists as well as what they did (*Los Angeles Times*, March 5, 1993, p. A20).

Reasons for Negative Portrayal of Islam by the Media

Many researchers -- Ghareeb (1983), Haddad (1991), Said (1987), and Lee (1991), among others -- have analyzed the reasons for biased coverage. These include: 1)cultural bias; 2)the conflict between Arabs and Israel; 3)the media's lack of information about the history of the conflict between Arabs and Israel; 4) the political power of the pro-Israel lobby and its influence over the American media; 5) the secular bias of the media; and 6) the new technological capabilities of the media.

Cultural, religious, or other civilizational differences are some of the many factors responsible for prejudice and conflict. It is natural to have different cultures at different times and places. However, it is not natural to develop cultural arrogance and a sense of civilizational superiority and hegemony. Arrogance, prejudice and hatred are mostly a product of ignorance. If many of us think that the world begins and ends within the United States of America, we will tend to look down on others, especially on those others whom we perceive as being hostile to us.

In one of my classes on international press and foreign media, students were surprised to learn that some of the so- called Third World countries also publish newspapers with comparable size, quality, and circulation to U. S. newspapers. For some students it was difficult to believe. Islam, with 1400 years of history, has its own cultural traditions. Lack of Islamic cultural perspectives leads people to perceive some Islamic traditions as being hostile to the West or Western traditions.

Lee (1991) describes the basis of this hostility by suggesting that, "Western nations live in a culture of war. How can the media play a role which is constructively critical of the State and which contributes directly to a culture of peace? " Media play a constant and illusory role in people's lives, argues Lee. Newspapers, television, magazines, comics, videos, and computer games reinforce any image that fits the culture of war at a given time. There was a time when "Cold War" rhetoric was so powerful that millions of Americans firmly believed that the USSR was capable and ready to over-run Europe and America. Now it is the turn of Islam and Muslims. If it is true that we can not live without having a major enemy or a major global threat, then perhaps Islamic fundamentalism or Islam is the easy, natural and only choice after the fall of communism in the USSR and Eastern Europe.

Suleiman (1983) supports this argument by contending that an important reason for negative portrayal of Muslims and Islam in the media is the fear of Islam and the Muslims by the West. This fear is unfortunately reinforced by Western scholars and so-called experts on Arabs and Islam in the West. Immediately after the arrest of Mohammad Salmeh, the World Trade Center Bombing suspect, a University of Miami expert on the Middle East and terrorism remarked during a CNN newscast that the real issue in the Middle East is not the Arab-Israeli conflict, but the threat of Islamic fundamentalism. This and many similar discourses, on American radio and television, by the so-called experts and analysts show a deliberate attempt to present Islam as the enemy of the West, especially America. Most media rely on such uninformed or prejudiced sources.

The cover of *The Atlantic Monthly* magazine (September, 1990) presents a picture of a Muslim, the follower of Islam. This picture (see next page) suggests many things, including that the followers of Islam are nomads, barbaric, and full of anger and vengeance. That is what most students said when this author showed the cover picture to students in one of his senior-level journalism classes. This cover, along with the article, "The

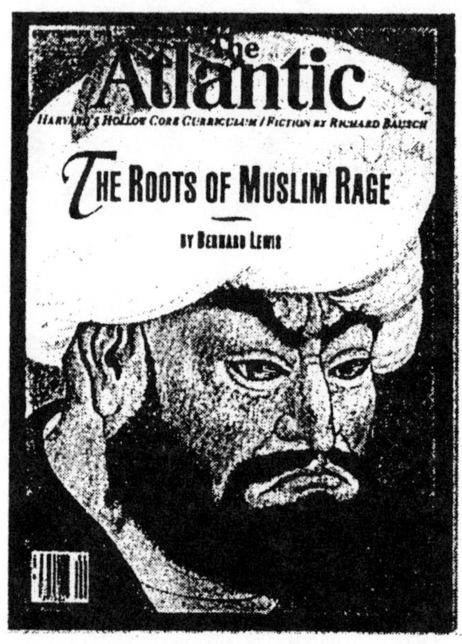

Roots of Muslim Rage," that appeared in the magazine, serves no other purpose than misinforming the readers and scaring them of the second largest religion of the world.

The Arab-Israeli conflict plays an important role in shaping Islamic images. The way media portray Arabs and the policies of the U. S. administration make Israel the most trusted friend and the Arabs, and consequently Islam, the most hated enemy.

After analyzing the impact of American foreign policy in the Middle East on the identity of Arab Muslims in the United States, Haddad (1991) notes, "A major element in the experience of the Muslim community in the United States during the last forty years has been a rising sense of hypocrisy of succeeding presidential administrations. Muslims feel they are living in a country that is hostile not only to their ethnic origins, but increasingly to Islam and Muslims in general (p.223)."

Many reporters follow the approach adopted by the administration. Mughees--uddin (1993), after analyzing *The New York Times*, the *Washington Post*, and the *Los Angeles Times,* has concluded that most media follow and support the administration's approach in foreign policy issues related to Muslims and Islam.

The secular bias of the media is yet another important factor. Muslims suffer more than any other religious group because of Islam's emphasis on the unity of religion and state. The secular bias, combined with the market-oriented goals of the media industry and political and corporate pressures on the media, often make it very difficult for the media to exercise self restraint and adhere to the notion of social responsibility.

Most media practitioners are unable to understand and appreciate why Muslims see things in a holistic world view of Islam, rather than a compartmentalized and fragmented "World Order." Clifford Christians (1987) advocates moral reasoning to minimize the secular bias and profit motives. He contends that the social responsibility of the media does not just lie in placing the ethics of truth-telling, human dignity and solidarity with the weak above the need to make a profit. It is also a matter of acting independently of social and political restraints which are contrary to universal human values such as justice and peace. Christians observes that, "in a frenzied world, how can 'obligation to truth' or 'comprehensive coverage of minority groups' hope to hold on its own against 'get the quote' and shoot the 'tear-jerking photo'? How can truth-telling be allowed to give a competitor an advertising edge? How can respect for the elderly be written into television comedy? Somewhere in the sorting out of these media imperatives, a practitioner must begin to assign priorities and then live by them. That process is called moral reasoning. We contend that the journalists, advertising executives, and entertainment programmers should be among the best trained moral thinkers in the land."

Another factor which is mostly ignored by many researchers is the technological capability of media to manipulate and create pseudo-contexts in which events can be easily removed from their real contexts and presented in any manner that is dictated either by the competitive necessity or by the profit motive. The Pentagon production, "Operation Desert Storm," and the mid-air shooting of the Iranian jetliner are among the best examples of a pseudo-context in a technological order detached from democratic accountability and set free from moral restraints (Phelon, 1991).

Thus, Islam is seen as a threat to the modern civilization and culture. Many Americans perceive Islam to be incompatible with the modern way of living. Violence and Islam are closely related to each other. There are a good many people, as noted by many analysts and scholars, who think that the war between communism and the West is about to be replaced by a war between the West and Muslims. It is very alarming to note that so many Americans seem to think that the next major war will be fought between the followers of Islam and the West. Let us hope that our view of Islam becomes more complex and comprehensive as we learn more about Muslims and Islam. Let us hope, as John Spayde (1994) observes that, "A faith that is professed by the fundamentalist misogynists in Iran and Egypt, feminists in Morocco and England, taxi drivers and kings in Ghana, Nigeria, and Kenya, office workers in Malaysia, nuclear scientists in Kazakhstan, martyrs in Bosnia -- and more than six million Americans -- is as far beyond stereotyping as humanity itself."

Contrary to the hostile picture of Islam, "The word Islam comes from the three-letter root word in Arabic 'slm,' which stands for peace as," notes Haddad (*USA Today,* 1993, March 10). "Islam," she says, "is the religion of peace. That's the way Koran talks about it -- the religion of peace. When you become a Muslim, you become at peace with God. And, that's what Islam means, to surrender to God, to stop fighting God . . . People should know that Islam, in a sense, urges people to worship the same God that Christianity and Judaism do."

References

Bodansky, Yossef and Vaughan Forrest (1990, March). A Question of Trust. U. S. House of Representatives House Republicans Task Force on Terrorism and Unconventional Warfare, Washington, DC.

______________________(1992, September). Iran's European Spring Board. U. S. House of Representatives House Republicans Task Force on Terrorism and Unconventional Warfare, Washington, DC.

Esposito, John L. (1992). *The Islamic Threat: Myth or Reality*? New York: Oxford University Press.

Ghareeb, E. (1983). A Renewed Look at the American Coverage of the Arabs: Toward a Better Understanding, in E. Ghareeb (ed.) *Split Vision, the Portrayal of Arabs in the American Media*. Washington, D. C.: American Arab Affairs Council: 157-194.

Haddad, Yvonne Yazbeck (1991). *The Muslims of America*. New York: Oxford University Press.

Lee, Philip (1991). Images of a Culture of War. *Media Development*, v. 4: 12-15,

Lewis, Bernard (1990, September). The Roots of Muslim Rage. *The Atlantic Monthly*: 47-60.

Michener, James A. (1955, June). Islam; The Misunderstood Religion. *Reader's Digest*: 77-85.

Mughees-uddin (1993). Many Voices One Chorus: Framing Islam and Islamic Movements (FIS and Hamas) in the US. Elite Press (*The New York Times, The Washington Post and The Los Angeles Times)*. Paper presented at the First Conference of the North American Association of Muslim Professionals and Scholars, Chicago, April 9-11.

Nelan, Bruce W. (1993, October 4) . The Dark Side of Islam. Time: 62-63.

Patai, Raphael. (1981, December 6). Violence, The Islamic Curse. *Chicago Tribune*.

Pipes, Daniel (1992, October 30). Fundamental Questions About Muslims. *The Wall Street Journa*l.

Perlmutter, Amos (1993, January 22). Islamic Fundamentalist Network. *The Washington Times*.

Said E. W. (1987). The MESA Debate: The Scholars, the Media and the Middle East. *Journal of Palestine Studies,* v. 16 (2): 85-104.

Spayde, Jon (1994, March/April). Islam. *Utne Reader*: 76.

Steinfles, Peter (1993, March 8). Like Islam, Its Fundamentalism has many Forums. *The New York Times*: A11

'Suleiman, M. W. (1965). An Evaluation of the Middle East News Coverage in Seven American News Magazines, July- December , 1965. *Middle East Forum,v.* 41: 9-30.

Zuckerman, Mortimer B. (1993, March 22). Beware of Religious Stalinists. *U. S. News & World Report,* Editorial: 22.

CHAPTER THREE

Muslims and Media

TO Create an Enemy

Start with an empty canvas.
Sketch in broad outlines the forms of
men, women, and children.

Dip into the unconscious well of your own
disowned darkness with a wide brush and
stain the stranger with a sinister hue of the shadow.

Trace on the face of the enemy the greed, hatred, carelessness
you dare not claim as your own.

Obscure the sweet individuality of each face.

Erase all hints of the myriad loves, hopes, fears that play
through the kaleidoscope of every finite heart.

Twist the smile until it forms the downward arc of cruelty.

Strip flesh from bone until only the abstract skeleton of
death remains.

Exaggerate each feature until man is metamorphosed into
beast, vermin, insect.

Fill in the background with malignant figures from ancient
nightmares--devils, demons, myrmidons of evil.

When your icon of the enemy is complete,
you will be able to kill without guilt,
slaughter without shame.

The thing you destroy will have become
merely an enemy of God, an impediment
to the sacred dialectic of history."

--Sam Keen (1986). *Faces of the Enemy*. Harper & Row: 9.

The media portrayal of Muslims very much fits the above description of how an enemy can be created. The American media pundits never let go off an opportunity to tell their audiences that the Muslims are anti-modern, uncivil and anti-West.

The front cover of the *National Review* of November 19, 1990, carries pictures of Muslim warriors riding camels with a caption in bold letters: "The Muslims are coming, The Muslims are coming." This stereotypical image of Muslims is very frightening for Americans, most of whom did not know enough about Muslims in order to form an opinion based on their own judgment.

While media have always pointed out that "Muslim men" were implicated in the World Trade Center bombing, never did the media say that the suspects in Oklahoma City bombing were Christians. The media completely failed to take note when a million-dollar newly built mosque in California was burnt and completely destroyed on September 1, 1994. Similarly, the media failed to report the arson of a New York City mosque. One should read the above quotation from Sam Keens' book and analyze how the enemy is being created and how the distance between "us" and "them" is enlarged.

Daniel Pipes, director of the Foreign Policy Institute in Philadelphia, expresses concern about the stubborn record of Muslims' illiteracy. Pipes (1990) notes that, "the key issue is whether Muslims will modernize . . . Should they fail to modernize, their stubborn record of illiteracy, poverty, intolerance, and autocracy will continue, or perhaps worsen."

It is not clear in what way Muslims have failed to modernize. Does modern mean acceptance and practice of the culture and values of the West, or is it meant to say that as long as Muslims follow Islam they can not modernize? The statement by Pipes also suggests that Muslims are intolerant and autocratic. Muslims are in power in more than forty countries in Asia, Africa and Europe. Is it fair to generalize their behavior based on the example of one or two Muslim governments? Muslims have welcomed, cooperated, interacted and worked with people of other faiths during the climax of their power in Spain and the Middle East. For over a century, Basra, now in Iraq, was the international center of learning. Scholars and students from all over the world used to travel to Basra to learn the science of astronomy, chemistry, and mathematics. Muslims themselves have traveled to the farthest distances such as China in the East, Greece and Portugal in the West, and many cities in Central Asia to learn the contemporary sciences and arts. Muslims, Jews and Christians have lived peacefully for centuries in the Middle East, especially in the Palestine-Israel region (Chacour, 1984). It is true that there have been wars among Muslims, Christians and Jews, and it is also true that there are some basic differences in religious thoughts and practices between Muslims and non-Muslims. However, let us not forget that there have been wars among many people and many nations throughout human history. From the ancient wars to the holocaust, and from the American-Japanese conflict to the war in Vietnam, human history is filled with conflict and confrontation based on religious, political, and cultural differences. We will better serve ourselves and the world if we focus on points of similarity than picking on points of difference, conflicts, and confrontation.

As a result of media stereotyping, Muslims are the first suspect in a crisis situation. The bombing of the Murrah Federal Building in Oklahoma City on April 19, 1995, is a good example. Immediately after the bomb blast, radio and television started reporting that people of

Middle Eastern origin were the prime suspects. Expert after expert, including one congressman, appeared on television and radio talk shows supporting the idea that suspects were of Middle Eastern origin. *Chicago Tribune* columnist, late Mike Royko, joined the bandwagon and wrote on April 21, 1995, "President Clinton says we should be cautious about placing blames or taking action. O.K. But when the time comes for punishment, it wouldn't be an eye for eye. That's just a swap. We should take both eyes, ears, nose, the entire anatomy. That's how to make a lasting impression." Looking at Royko's columns after the suspects were arrested and found to be white, Christians, and from the Midwest, not from the Middle East, one could not find any impatient appeal for a swift action. Royko obviously calmed down after finding out that the suspects were one of his own. However, Muslims suffered through out the nation.

In all of 1991, just 119 hate crimes against Arabs and Muslims were reported in the U. S., even though the Gulf War occurred during this period. In three days immediately following the Oklahoma City blast, more than 227 hate crimes against Muslims were reported (CAIR, 1995). A hate crime, as defined in a document issued by the U. S. Department of Justice in 1993, is a criminal offense committed against a person or property which is motivated, in whole or in part, by the offender's bias against a race, religion, ethnic/national origin group, or sexual orientation. What Muslims experienced after the Oklahoma City bombing may well be categorized as hate crimes. Included in this were hate calls to individual Muslims as well as Islamic Centers, stalking, false arrests, police harassment, verbal threats, death and bomb threats, beating and physical assaults, and shootings. The environment of hate and suspicion significantly affected the daily life of Muslims. Many Muslim businesses experienced a substantial decrease in the number of customers. Muslim women wearing Islamic dress and school-going children suffered most, as they were afraid to go out during the first few days after the bombing. A Muslim woman in her mid 20s miscarried her near-term baby after an attack on her house in Oklahoma City on April 20, 1995. The Islamic Center at High Point, North Carolina, was burnt to ground on the early morning of April

26, 1995. A seventh-grade Muslim student at the Richardson Middle School in Torrence, California, was slandered with words such as "camel jockey" and assaulted physically after her English teacher included the word "bomb" in students' vocabulary and used it in a sentence, "Muslims bombed Oklahoma City because Allah told them to do so." (CAIR, 1995). "We were held hostage for 72 hours," said the leader of Momin Mosque in Oklahoma City.

The media played a significant role in spreading the rumor, and consequently provoking Americans to think that after the World Trade Center bombing Muslim terrorists had struck in the American heartland. Within minutes of the bombing, a local TV station started broadcasting that the Nation of Islam was responsible for this attack. A couple of hours later they reported that the FBI was looking for three men of Middle Eastern origin (*Impact*: May 1995). CNN was the first network to broadcast an interview with former Congressman David McCurdy on April 19, 1995. McCurdy noted that, "there could be a very real connection to some of the Islamic fundamentalist groups that have actually been operating out of Oklahoma City." On the same day Steven Emerson, producer of the PBS documentary, "Jihad in America," declared on the CBS Evening News: "Oklahoma City, I can tell you, is probably considered as one of the largest centers of Islamic radical activity outside the Middle East." A former Congressman and a so-called expert on terrorism were the most widely quoted sources of allegation that the bombing was done by Muslim terrorists. John McWeathy reported on ABC World News, April 19: "Sources say that FBI has been watching dozens of suspicious Islamic groups in cities in the Southwest and several in Oklahoma City." Jim Cumins, on NBC Nightly News, April 19, compared the bombing to that in Beirut. On April 20, Laryy Johnson, identified as an international security expert, said in an interview with Robert MacNeil of PBS, "The threat [of terrorism] has narrowed -- in that it is focused more on Islamic groups."

Radio talk shows took upon themselves to inflame the hatred against Muslims. Here is an excerpt from the Bob Grant Show on WABC, New York, April 20: "A Caller: 'Well, I'd like to say that it's very amazing that . . . they're talking about Muslims and Mr. Salameh and all this, this is what you are saying, and no one ever saw anything. That's just as worse--; Grant: Now -- yeah -- we did see a lot of things... In the Oklahoma case . . . the indications are that those people who did it were some Muslim terrorists. But, a skunk like you, what I'd like to do is put you up against the wall with the rest of them, and mow you down along with them. Execute you with them."

Looking at newspapers, one finds that most, including *The New York Times, USA Today, Washington Post,* and *Chicago Tribune* were instrumental in adding to the confusion. *The Post* wrote on April 20, "The FBI has been aware of the activity of Islamic groups meeting recently in Oklahoma City, Dallas, and Kansas." On April 20, *USA Today* quoted, Daniel Pipes, editor of *Middle East Quarterly*. Pipes said, "People need to understand that this is just the beginning. The fundamentalists are on the upsurge, and they make it very clear that they are targeting us. They are absolutely obsessed with us." After an Arab-Muslim was detained at London's Heathrow Airport and sent back to the U. S. for questioning, *The Daily Telegraph* ran this front page headline: "Oklahoma bomb suspect seized at Heathrow,"

It is evident from above examples that it was not merely a criticism of "Muslim extremists" or "Muslim fundamentalists," rather it was an outright defamation of the entire Muslim community. Was it sufficient to infer criminality, as *The New York Times* (April 20, 1995) did, from the mere presence of Islamic religious institutions in Oklahoma City? Even after the possibility of Muslim or Arab involvement was ruled out by the authorities, some media sources insisted on maintaining Muslims' link to the bombing. CNN's Wolf Blitzer, on April 20, insisted that, "there is still a possibility that there could have been some sort of connection to Middle East terrorism." Wolf Blitzer was quoted on April 21 in *The Cincinnati Post,* which went a step further in quoting an unidentified law enforcement source that a Muslim cab driver from New York, Asad R. Siddiqy, arrived in Oklahoma City an hour before the blast, and is considered a suspect. The paper even published a photograph of Siddiky.

In a journalism class of mostly seniors, when this author asked about who were the t errorists, students had only one answer: "They are the Muslims from the Middle East." This mythical image of Muslim terrorism is perpetuated by the media, which relies on a number of terrorism experts who seem to have their own political agenda.

According to a 1993 FBI report on domestic terrorist acts (FBI: 1995), radicals from Muslim background carried out only one terrorist attack in the United States -- The World Trade Center bombing. In contrast, 77 terrorist attacks involved Puerto Ricans, 23 attacks involved left-wing groups, 16 attacks involved Jewish groups, 12 attacks involved anti-Castro Cubans, and six terrorist attacks involved right-wing groups. Similarly with regard to the terrorist attacks against the United States overseas, the Department of State (1995) in its report, "Pattern of Global Terrorism," noted that a majority of 44 anti-US. attacks in 1994 took place in Latin America, whereas, eight were carried out in the Middle East, five in Asia, five in Western Europe, and four in Africa.

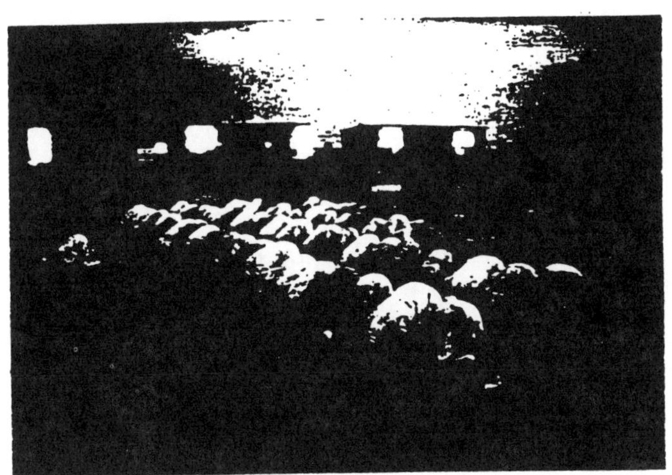

AT PRAYER: Sudanese in an alliance of ideology and convenience with Iran.

In a story on Sudan, a country in Africa that the US. has categorized as a terrorist state, *Time* magazine (August 30, 1993) used a picture of the Muslims (see above) while they were praying. The caption on this picture reads: "At Prayer: Sudanese in Alliance of Ideology and

Convenience with Iran." The *Time* reporter created a new symbol for the world to hate: Muslims performing their obligatory five daily prayers in congregation. Millions of *Time*'s readers will now associate this image with terrorists.

In the World Trade Center (WTC) bombing, 15 Muslims were indicted in August of 1993. American Muslims' response was quick, and clear. On March 4, 1993, at news conferences in Washington, D. C., New York, and Los Angeles, Muslim leaders condemned the bombing. In a statement published in *Los Angeles Times* (March 5, 1993) Muslim leaders of the United States and Canada made it clear that, "Any practicing Muslim would definitely be against any acts of terrorism against anyone -- Jews, Christians or Muslims -- It is quite honest to admit that among Muslims, just like among Christians and Jews, there are elements that are extremists. They are elements on the fringe."

The 15 persons indicted in the WTC bombing were not a part of any close-knit organization. The Blind Muslim cleric, Sheikh Omar Abdul Rahman, was not even known to most Muslims in the United States. He was never invited to speak at any of the national Islamic conventions in the US. or Canada, yet many media outlets portrayed the entire Muslim community to be part of a "grand Islamic conspiracy." Headlines such as " Islam: Terror Strikes Again" and "Bombs in the Name of Allah," were published associating Islam and Allah (Islamic equivalent of God) with terror, violence and bomb.

Muslims were shocked and surprised to note that in one of the most popular Disney movies for children, *The Lion King*, when the evil-natured hyenas were shown, a crescent appears on the horizon. The crescent has been used as an Islamic symbol in many of the Muslim arts and paintings. Equating darkness and evil with Islam is yet another way to dehumanize Muslims and portray them as enemies.

This treatment of Muslims by the media is due mainly to the perception of many Americans, including media practitioners, that Islam is anti-West, in particular anti-American. It is true that many events, especially the revolution in Iran in 1979, the World Trade Center bombing in 1993, and the bombing in Riyadh, Saudi Arabia in

November, 1995, encourage one to think that it is Islamic to be anti-American. However, more than anti-Americanism, these events reflect the political instability, deprivation of basic human rights in many of the Muslim countries supported by the U. S. administration, and an exploitation of these countries' resources to the advantage of a royal family of kings, amirs, presidents, and dictators.

"Muslims can not be anti-Western because Islam is pro not anti any region or its people," noted Hasan Turabi, Secretary General of the Popular Arab and Islamic Conference (*Impact*, May 1995). Today, many Americans hate Iran which was the closest American ally among the Muslim governments during the regime of the Shah of Iran. At that time Iran received most favorable treatment by the then U. S. government and the media, both of which ignored the human rights abuses by the Shah and the potential of the Shah's religious and political opposition. A similar situation exists now in many of Muslim countries, including Algeria, Egypt, Kuwait, and Saudi Arabia, where hundreds of Muslims are behind bars, many have disappeared and no one knows about their whereabouts, and many have been even hanged. Most of these Muslims are professionals, scholars, diplomats, and authors, yet the media portray them as terrorists and fundamentalists and ignore the popular unrest that exists in these countries. "Much of the unprecedented wealth from oil revenues has been squandered on an unprecedented scale, in an unprecedented style . . . Lawyers and journalists are unable to work freely . . . The increasing stridency in their (Muslims) tone is thus linked to the larger Muslim sense of anger and powerlessness." (*Utne Reader*, March/April 1994: 84)

With the support of the U. S. government, and with positive publicity given by the American media, many of the rulers in the above mentioned Muslim countries are becoming more repressive towards their own people, leading to more Americans targeted for revenge. The bombing of a building in Riyadh, Saudi Arabia, on November 13, 1995, in which seven Americans were killed, is an example of how anger and frustration against one's own government is directed towards Americans when people discover that Americans are the ones on whose strong support their corrupt and unpopular governments are functioning.

Another reason of the prejudice and unfair treatment of Muslims by the media is, as some researchers and analysts (Abuljobain, 1993) believe, the presence of a strong anti-Muslim Zionist lobby that controls most of the media and influences the legislators at state capitols and in Washington, D. C. These researchers assert that the majority of the American media practitioners adopt the line of argument advanced by powerful interest groups who support the government of Israel.

A series of reports published by the House Republicans Task Force in 1990, 1992 and 1993 ferociously attack Muslims and hold them responsible for terrorist attacks against U. S. (Bodansky, Yossef and Vaughan Forrest, 1990, 1992). Many Muslims see the 1995 Omnibus Counter-Terrorism Act as an attempt by the above mentioned groups to undermine Muslims' religious freedom in America. The legislation, signed by President Clinton in April 1996, has been widely condemned by Muslim organizations all across America. Twenty major Muslim organizations issued a signed statement asking the members of Congress and Senate to oppose measures that will presumably violate basic rights to free speech and religious practices. While some have compared it with the principle of guilt by association that defined the McCarthy era (David Cole, 1995), others have looked at it as the mockery of democracy in America where "Rule number one is that everyone is equal under the law; and rule number two is that the government will determine to whom Rule number one applies." (*Impact*: May 1995).

One important reason for the negative media coverage of Muslims is their own lack of interaction with and participation in the media. Muslims have long seen the media as an arch enemy, a conspirator and a blasphemer, and rarely tried to establish a mutually beneficial relationship with the media. Consequently, neither the Muslims nor the media are comfortable with each other.

"If Islam is put into an American context," Said Salam Al-Marayati, Director of the Los Angeles based Muslim Public Affairs Council, "then it will emerge as a valuable element of American pluralism . . . Being Muslim does make one different, but there is so much that Muslims can share with other Americans." (Al-Marayati, 1995).

Only when Muslims understand the nature of American pluralism as well as the power dynamics in America, will they be able to get more positive coverage from the media. "Any group that projects itself as a threatening group is humiliated," said Maher Hathout, a cardiologist and President of the Islamic Center of Southern California in Los Angeles. He asserted that, "there is a part played by media and others, but a great part of the fear in this society's mind comes from what we say and what we do. If we continue to allow ourselves to be projected as a frightening group, it will be very detrimental for the future of Islam in America. American society does not mind if you are liberal or conservative, but they do not like when they feel scared. The experience of the Black Panther or Waco group is very relevant." (Hathout, 1995).

Emphasizing Muslims' active interaction with media, Hathout (1993) observed that, "ignorance is the breeding home of fear, anxieties and prejudice. People are always afraid of things they don't know."

"Blaming others, the media, and living under the conspiracy theory are very detrimental to Muslims' growth in American society," said Fayyaz Khan, former editor of the New York-based Muslim monthly magazine, *The Message International.* "The victim syndrome is the loser syndrome," noted Khan (1995). He summarized Muslims' future strategy in dealing with the media by reading an anonymous quotation: "The best defense is not defense. The best defense is not offense. The best defense is compassion and confidence."

References

AbulJobain, Ahmad (1993). *Radical Islamic Terrorism or Political Islam*? Annandale, VA: United Association for Studies and Research, Occasional Paper Series No. 1.

Al-Marayati, Salam (1995). Quotation from personal interview given to this author, (January 21).

Bodansky, Yousef and Vaughn Forrest (March 1, 1990). US House of Representatives. House of Representative Research Committee. *A Question of Trust*. Washington, D. C. : Task Force on Terrorism and Unconventional warfare: 2.

_______________ *Iran's European Springboard*. Ibid. (September 1, 1992:1).

_______________ *The New Islamist International* (February 1, 1993: 65).

CAIR (1995). *A Rush to Judgment* (A Special Report on Anti-Muslim Stereotyping, Harassment and Hate Crimes Following the Bombing of Oklahoma City's Murrah Federal Building, April 19, 1995). Washington, DC.: Council on American Islamic Relations (CAIR).

Chacour, Elias and David Hazard (1984). *Blood Brothers*. Grand Rapids, Michigan: Chosen Books.

Cole, David (1995). As quoted by Rafique Mirza in *Impact*, May 1995: 8-9.

Federal Bureau of Investigation (1995). Terrorist Research and Analytical Section's Report.

Grant, Bob (1995). Bob Grant Show on WABC, New York, April 20, as quoted by the CAIR: op. cit.,: 6.

Hathout, Maher (1995). Quotation from interview given to this author (January 21).

Impact (May 1995). Targeting Islam, targeting America: 8-9.

Impact (May 1995). Polite Engagement is an Unilateral Islamic Obligation: 14-15.

Keen, Sam (1986). *Faces of the Enemy: Reflections of the Hostile Imagination*. New York: Harper and Row.

Khan, Fayyaz (1994). Quotation from an interview given to this author (November 21).

Los Angeles Times (March 5, 1993). U. S. Islamic Leaders Condemn Bombing, Brace for Backlash: A20.

Pipes, Daniel (1990). The Muslims are Coming, The Muslims are Coming. *National Review*, November 19: 28-31.

Royko, Mike (1995). Time to up the Ante Against Terrorism. *Chicago Tribune*, April 21.

The Cincinnati Post (April 21, 1995). Face of Terrorist?. pages 1A, 3A, 6A, and 9A.

The U. S. Department of State (19950. *Pattern of Global Terrorism,* Washington, D. C.: U. S. government Printing Office.

Time (August 30, 1993). Is Sudan Terrorism's New Best Friend: 30-31.

Utne Reader (March April 1994). Terror and Tolerance, Muslims Rage at the West is Justified-But it is not Islamic: 81-84.

CHAPTER FOUR

UNDERSTANDING ISLAM

Today an estimated six million Muslims (Shaikh, 1992, Husain, 1996) live in the United States, yet Islam is still one of the most misunderstood religions in this country. What many Americans know about Islam and Muslims is a series of clichés. Most Americans don't know anything about Islam, and their only source of information about Islam is the media. According to a *Time* (April 6, 1993) magazine survey, sixty four percent of those surveyed were not aware or did not know anything about Islam. The purpose of this chapter is to present a brief and simple account of Islam's beliefs and practices for the benefit of the general readers and particularly for media practitioners who write on Islam. Many reporters, who write about Islam and with whom this author has met, expressed that a brief and simple account of Islam from a Muslim perspective will help media practitioners to have a better understanding of Islam.

Islam is not a new religion, but the same truth that God revealed through all His prophets to every people. For about a billion Muslims, Islam is both a religion and a complete way of life. The word Islam comes from the three-letter root word in Arabic "slm," which means peace. Submission and obedience to God bring peace: peace with one's own self; peace with God; and peace with people and everything else that exists in the world. Islam is the name of the monotheistic religion based on the belief that, "there is no god but Allah and Muhammad is His messenger."

Allah is the Arabic word for one God. Allah is not God of Muslims alone, He is God of all people and other creations. Islam, as Qur'an (the book revealed by God to Muhammad) describes, is the religion revealed to all the prophets including Abraham, the prophet who submitted to the will of God and in whose family are the prophets Moses, Jesus, and Muhammad (Qur'an -- 3: 83, 84). Islam is sometimes incorrectly called "Mohammedanism" and the Muslims as "Mohammedans." Unlike Christianity, Judaism, Buddhism, and many other religions, Islam has not been named after Muhammad. He was not the founder of Islam; he did not start a new religion. The name Islam is given to this religion by God. The Qur'an says, "surely, the way of life acceptable to God is Islam" (3: 19). "He (God) named you Muslims before and in this (Qur'an)" (22: 78).

Qur'an is a record of the exact words revealed by God through the Angel Gabriel to the Prophet Muhammad. The revelation, or the communication of God's will to human beings (Al Faruqi, 1986: 95), began in 610 CE when Muhammad was forty years old, and lasted until his death 23 years later. It was memorized by Muhammad and then dictated to his companions, and written down by scribes, who cross-checked it during his lifetime. Every single word of the 114 chapters (surah), consisting of 6, 616 verses (ayat); 77, 934 words; and 323, 671 letters, is considered to be the exact word of God. Muslims believe the Qur'an to be the last word of God who Himself has taken the responsibility of preserving it (Qur'an 15:9). The historicity and integrity of the text of the Qur'an stands absolutely beyond question (Al-Faruqi, 1986: 101).

Qur'an is the prime source of Muslims' faith and practice. As final revelation, Qur'an is also considered to be the culmination and completion of God's guidance to human beings. It also reaffirms and confirms the true teachings of Torah, Psalms, the Gospels, and other revealed scriptures (Qur'an -- 6:92; 5:46, 48). Qur'an focuses on guiding principles for human beings and relegates to them the task of translating these principles into a plan of action for daily living. Thus, while the basic principles will remain the same through different time and places, the derivation in the form of law will be different according to the needs of society.

God himself is at the very center of ideas in Qur'an. His being one, that is Tawhid, is the basic theme of Qur'an (Sarwar, 1987:33). Surrounding this central theme, Qur'an reflects upon a number of basic principles (Al-Faruqi, 1986: 109-110) which guide human beings in their dealings with God and the world in which they live: 1) Rationalism is a key principle referring to the subjection of all knowledge, including religious knowledge, to the dictates of reason and common sense; 2) Humanism is yet another basic theme of Qur'an. It means that all human beings are born innocent, equal, capable of making judgment of truth and falsehood, accountable before God for their actions, and free to determine their individual destinies; 3)God created this life to be lived and enjoyed, and not to be destroyed and denied. There is an order and a purpose in the creation of this world and human beings are charged with the responsibility of fulfilling that purpose and maintaining that order; 4) Human beings are socially responsible. Even though their individual self is fully recognized and respected by God, their worth is in their membership and contributions to the society they live in.

The original text of Qur'an is in the Arabic language. Qur'an has so far been translated into more than one hundred languages. However, the original text, in most cases, accompanies the translation.

Traditions of Prophet Muhammad (Sunnah) means a path or an example worthy of following. Sunnah is embodied in Hadith, which refers to the sayings, actions, and whatever was approved by Muhammad. Sunnah and Hadith are the second most significant source of authority for Muslims. Hadith is considered to be the first and most authentic commentary of Qur'an. A rigorous scientific method of authentication was developed to determine the authenticity of more than 600,000 sayings of Muhammad. During the first three centuries after the death of Muhammad, many great Muslim scholars (Bukhari, d. 870 CE; Muslim, d. 875 CE; Abu Dawud, d. 888 CE; al-Tirmidhi, d. 892 CE; Ibn Ma'ja, d. 896 CE; and al-Nisai, d. 915 CE) compiled different collections of Hadith. The six canonical collections of Hadith which were accepted through the Islamic history by Sunni Muslims (Nasr, 1993:19) contain more than 10,000 authentic Hadith. A century later, Shiite scholars also compiled four books of authentic Hadiths. The content of most of the Hadiths in the two collections is basically the same; it is the chain of transmission which differs in many cases (Nasr, Ibid.). Almost all Muslim scholars, in all ages, have agreed that without the help of Hadith, Qur'an can not be fully understood and appreciated.

Islam 's basic beliefs: 1)Oneness of God; 2) Angels of God; 3) Books of God; 4) Messengers of God; 5) The Day of Judgment; 6) The life hereafter; and 7) Predestination or supremacy of the divine will (Sarwar, 1987:18). These seven beliefs can be grouped into three cardinal elements of Islamic belief: 1) Tawhid (Oneness of

God); 2) Risalah (Prophethood); and 3) Akhirah (the life hereafter.

Tawhid means oneness of God. It is the essence of Islam: the act of affirming God to be the one, absolute, transcendent creator, lord and master of all that is. Simply expressed, Tawhid is the conviction and witnessing that "there is no god but God." It is acceptance of the supremacy of God's will, and it provides a basis for Islamic moral and ethical foundations. It affirms that God, being beneficent and purposive, did not create human beings in vain. Instead, they have been obligated to prove themselves as being morally worthy. Tawhid provides human beings with a universal vision and elevates them above narrow and sectarian prejudices of color, race, language and even religion.

Prophethood refers to the acceptance of all the messengers of God including Adam, Noah, Abraham, Moses, Jesus, and Muhammad as His chosen people to bring God's guidance to human beings. Prophets were neither partners to God, nor did they share power with God; they were simply His messengers. All the prophets preached essentially the same basic message: Worship God, and there is no god but One God. God sent prophets to every nation at different times (Qur'an -- 10:47; 13:7; 35:24). The last in the chains of Prophets was Muhammad (Qur'an -- 33:40) in whom God completed His message to humanity which is contained in the last revelation, the Qur'an, and God's final message, Islam (Qur'an -- 5:3). Obedience to God is tied to the obedience of the Prophet.

Throughout the Islamic history, the message of Qur'an and the example of the Prophet Muhammad have constituted the formative and enduring foundation of the Islamic faith and belief (Esposito, 1988:360).

Muhammad was born in 570/571 CE in Makkah or Mecca, now in Saudi Arabia. His father, Abdullah, died before his birth, and Aminah, Muhammad's mother, died when he was six. He was brought-up first by his grandfather , Abdul Muttalib, and later by his uncle Abu Talib. Muhammad was still a boy when he worked as a shepherd. As he grew up, he joined his uncle in taking trading caravans out of Makkah. Later, he was employed by a wealthy woman, Khadija, who owned many trade caravans. Muhammad successfully led Khadija's trade caravans for a number of years. Khadija married Muhammad while he was 25 and she was 40 years old. Khadijah remained the only wife of Muhammad for 25 years until her death in 620 CE.

Muhammad married eight times after the death of Khadija. Except for his marriage with Aisha, daughter of his closest companion, Abu Bakr, all the other marriages were for political and social reasons (Al-Faruqi, 1986: 123). An example will illustrate: Sawdah was the Muslim wife of Sakran, one of the first converts to Islam. Muhammad married the couple when Sawdah converted to Islam. She had to run away from her non-Muslim family to avoid their vengeance. The same happened to Sakran. Muhammad sent both to Abyssinia. On their return, after a few years, Sakran died. Sawdah had to choose between staying in the streets or returning to her family and their retribution. Muhammad married Sawdah and gave her the protection she needed. He also set an example for other Muslims that their families will not be left helpless should they die while struggling to follow Islam. Except one son, Muhammad's four daughters and two sons were from his first wife Khadija. All his sons died in infancy. Muhammad had only two grand children, both sons of his daughter Fatima.

Muhammad proclaimed and Qur'an confirmed that he was illiterate. Although he did not go to a school or receive instructions from any person, he was known to be a man of great wisdom, honesty, courage, and integrity. People knew him as the most truthful and trustworthy person who would come forward to solve complex problems in simple ways. In Makkah Muhammad never bowed before the idols and remained away from the pagan way of life. Instead, he used to spend a lot of time meditating at the cave of Hira atop the Mountain of Light at the outskirts of Makkah.

Muhammad's thirteen years in Makkah, after the revelation began, were most dreadful. He and his companions were tortured, ridiculed, and insulted. At the peak of oppression, Muhammad, along with his companions and most of their families, migrated to Madinah, a town about 250 miles north of Makkah.

In Madinah Muhammad found a much less hostile environment. Many tribes of Madinah had made covenant with Muhammad to support him in his mission. Even the non-Muslim groups such as the Jews and the Christians entered into an agreement of peaceful co-existence with Muslims.

While making his best efforts to establish an Islamic society in Madinah, Muhammad fought three major battles against the enemies of Islam: the battle of Badr (624 CE), the battle of Uhad (625 CE), and the battle of Trenches (627 CE). Three years before his death Muhammad re-entered Makkah as a victorious leader of Islam, which by that time had emerged as the most formidable political power in peninsular Arabia and a religion whose followers were soon to spread the message in all corners of the globe. Muhammad died at the age of 63 in 632/33 CE after a brief illness. He was buried in the quarters of his wife Aisha.

Belief in the life hereafter is the third major belief of Islam. According to this belief, human life is not limited to the short span of earthly existence; there will be an eternal life for every individual after the day of judgment when the entire human race will be resurrected; every one will have to appear before God and will have to face the good or bad consequence of his or her deeds in this life. The good consequence will mean living in paradise for ever, and the bad consequences will mean going to hell either for a short time or for ever. The belief in human accountability to God makes life meaningful and differentiates human beings from inanimate objects; it keeps a person upright and good, and it is the most potent force for producing virtues on this earth. There can not be a greater instrument of moral reformation and good and sound character than the belief in the hereafter. Muslims believe that such a belief is a surest protection against deviation, corruption, crime, immorality and injustice. God affirms in Qur'an (75:3,4) that all human beings will be brought before Him after they will be reborn, and then everyone has to clear accounts before leaving God's presence.

Pillars of Faith are the framework for a Muslim life. These are the practical reflections of accepting the rationality of the above mentioned major beliefs: Oneness of God, prophethood and the life in the hereafter. The pillars of faith include: 1) Declaration of faith (Shahadah); 2) Five obligatory daily prayers (Salat); 3) Poor-due payments (Zakat); 4)Fasting during the entire month of Ramadan (Siyam); and 5) Pilgrimage to the House of God in Makkah at least once in a lifetime for those who can afford it.

Shahada, or the declaration of faith, is the beginning point of becoming a Muslim. It refers to the recitation, in Arabic, of the basic Islamic Creed or Kalimah which means in English, "There is no god but God and Muhammad is His messenger." This simple pronouncement in public is required to become a Muslim.

لَآ إِلٰهَ إِلَّا ٱللّٰهُ مُحَمَّدٌ رَّسُولُ ٱللّٰهِ

Lā ilāha illal lāhu muḥammadur rasūlul lāh.

The belief in one God is the pristine essence of Islam. The declaration of faith, however, starts with the negation or rejection of all other deities. It is important to note that worshipping one God liberates one from the slavery of all man-made gods. A direct relationship is established between a person and the Lord without any intercession or priest in between. The second part of this declaration emphasizes that being a Muslim also entails accepting the authority of Muhammad, a human being whom God chose as His last messenger.

Salat, or prayer, means obligatory prayers which are performed five times a day and are a means to establish direct link between a worshipper and God. Although it is preferred to offer these prayers in congregation, a Muslim may also pray individually. Prayers at fixed times have been enjoined by God on the believers (Qur'an -- 4:103). Prayers are said at dawn, noon, mid to late afternoon, sunset, and nightfall, determining the rhythm of the entire day. Muslims offer prayers facing Makkah, the city that houses the Kaa'ba, the house of God first built by Adam, and later by

Abraham. Kaa'ba was housed during the time of Muhammad in the Mosque al-Haram in Makkah, now known as the grand-Mosque in Makkah (see Exhibit 1) which can accommodate approximately 1.4 million worshippers at a time (Saudi Ministry of Information: 1994).

On every Friday the noon prayer is offered in congregation with a sermon (Khutba) just before the prayer. Friday prayer has special significance in the lives of Muslims whom God ordered to leave every other business and join the congregation on Friday at the time when the call is given (Qur'an -- 62:9). A call (Adhan) is given before each prayer in order to announce the time of the prayer.

Zakat signifies a very important concept: all things belong to God, and wealth is therefore held by human beings as trust. The word zakat mean both purification and growth. Wealth is purified by setting aside a portion for those in need. Each year every Muslim who possesses a minimum capital, either in assets or in cash, is required to pay two and a half percent of that capital to the needy and the poor. This is in addition to the voluntary charity that every Muslim is encouraged to pay at one's own convenience and will. Zakat is a reminder to each Muslim that God encourages an economic system in which capital should flow from the rich to the poor (Qur'an -- 59: 7), and should not be monopolized by the rich and powerful in a society. Zakat is neither general charity nor taxation, it is an act of worship.

Fasting for an entire month, from dawn to sunset during the 9th month of Islamic calendar, Ramadan, is required for every adult Muslim man and woman. It involves abstaining from food, drink or sexual relations while fasting. Those who are sick, elderly, travelers, and women who are pregnant or nursing are permitted to break the fast and make up an equal number of days later in the year. If they are physically incapable of doing this, they must feed a needy person for each day missed. Muslims are expected to remain away from all bad actions during their fast. They should not tell a lie, break a promise, or do any deceitful act. The act of fasting makes a Muslim able to control the passions. It is considered to be an annual program of training and self-control in order to prepare a Muslim for true worship of God.

The month of Ramadan has special significance to Qur'an because the revelation contained in it was completed during this month. Recitation of the entire Qur'an is completed during the special prayers offered after the night prayer. Muslims devote special attention to learn, memorize and study Qur'an. The month of fasting is concluded with a grand celebration of Eid-ul-Fitr on the first day of the 10th month of the Islamic calendar. Eid-ul-Fitr is considered to be the most significant festival of Muslims.

Hajj is the annual pilgrimage to Makkah. It is an obligation for those who are physically and financially capable of doing it. Hajj is performed from the 8th to the 13th day of the last month of the Islamic calendar, Dhu'l Hijjah. The occasion provides an opportunity for about two million Muslims from all parts of the world to gather together for the sake of God. It is a unique experience for Muslims to come together in the service of God. Barriers of color, territory, language, race, and status disappear. Men wear two white cloths and women wear simple garments. The rites of Hajj include circling the house of God, Kaa'ba, seven times, and going seven times between the mountains of Safa and Marwa as did Hagar, the mother of Ishmael and wife of Abraham, during her search for water. Then the pilgrims stand together on the wide plain of Arafat and pray for forgiveness from God. The pilgrimage concludes with offering of a sheep, goat, or part of a camel or cow as sacrifice. This last act is to mark the great sacrifice for which Abraham readied himself when he offered his son Ishmael in the way of God. At the end Muslims, pilgrims and other Muslims all over the world, celebrate the festival of sacrifice, Eid-ul-Adha. Although not a part of Hajj, Muslims also visit the Mosque of Muhammad in Medinah and offer their respect and regard at the site of his grave.

Islam's world view is based on the above beliefs, principles, and concepts. Islam treats all human beings as one community which God created from a single male and a single female: Adam and Eve. There is no distinction and discrimination among them except that of righteousness and piety (Qur'an -- 49:13). Tawhid is the cornerstone of Islamic world view. God is sovereign, and human beings are God's deputy on this earth. A universal, peaceful society based on equality and justice is possible only through the fulfillment of God's mission: worship no god but God.

All aspects of life -- spiritual, cultural, social, economic, and political -- should be governed by God's law. Islamic world view opposes fragmentation and division on the basis of race, color, language, and even nationality. While the actualization of God's obedience will not be achieved through force, society will be encouraged to opt for good and abstain from evil. Freedom of expression and choice is an integral part of Islamic world view. God's mission can not be fulfilled by coercion or force. Peaceful dissent is to be allowed and protected by Islamic state. A non-Muslim may therefore become a citizen of an Islamic state and will be allowed to order his or her life under any system of law desired. In the Islamic state, where Islamic law is sovereign, Christian, Jewish, Hindu, and whatever other laws the non-Muslims wish to observe are permitted (Al-Faruqi, 1986: 160).

Islam considers God's guidance to be universal and dynamic. Human intellect is capable of relating this guidance to any time and place provided it accepts and surrenders to the Will of God. This acceptance of and surrender to the will of God is known as a dynamism that leads Muslims to develop jurisprudence, excel in medicine, astronomy, and mathematics, develop the rules of Islamic governance, and establish a just Islamic order. However, whenever Muslims are incapable of becoming dynamic and violate their trust with God, they lead to dictatorial societies, oppressive governments, and large-scale bloodshed and destruction.

Sharia means a path or a way to conduct life. It also means constitutional principles mandated by Qur'an and authenticated by the Sunnah of Muhammad. Muslims are obliged to strive for the implementation of Sharia (Qur'an -- 45:18). It is a source of law as well as moral guidance. Qur'an is a book of guidance; it does not provide a detailed account of law to govern various aspects of day-to-day life. It is the responsibility of the Muslim community and/or scholars to formulate laws that can effectively guide specific aspects of daily living.

The sources of law, in order of priority, are the Qur'an, the Sunnah, anological reasoning, and consensus. Many great jurists developed the jurisprudence (Fiqh) that are today known as the major schools of thought: Hanafi, Shafii, Maliki, Hanbali, and Jaafri. However, only Qur'an has divine status; Sharia should reflect the needs of time and place. Therefore, the formulation of Islamic laws (Sharia) is a dynamic process that requires creative interpretation (Ijtihad). The dynamism of Muslim society is dependent on the dynamism of Sharia. While the basic and fundamental guidance will remain the same, the laws dealing with contemporary human life should reflect the time-place element within the frame work of the divine guidance. The purpose of Sharia is to establish justice, equality among people, and prosperity in the land. If this purpose is not achieved, one should look into the Sharia and ask whether the incorporation of divine guidance is reflected in the Sharia or not? Unfortunately, Muslims' understanding of Sharia or the Islamic world view has been frozen in history (Sardar, 1991:224).

The history of Islam from the very beginning has been a history of Islam as a faith and as a political power. The small Islamic state in Madinah during the time and immediately after the death of Muhammad was an exemplification of how Islam nourished individual's faith and how it organized a Muslim community and a Muslim state.

After the death of Muhammad, Khilafah was the institution to manage the state of governance. It refers to the establishment of an Islamic state responsible 1)for the security and well being of its people, 2)for calling humanity to the submission of God's will, and 3) for the establishment of a new world order in which every human being can live in peace, improve in knowledge, share in God's bounty, and be free to convince and be convinced of the truth. The person who is chosen to lead the Khilafah is known as Khalifah (Caliph), or the leader: the head of the Islamic State.

After the death of Muhammad, the khilafah in its true sense continued for about 30 years with four Caliphs following one another as the leaders of the Islamic State: Abu Bakr, Umar, Uthman, and Ali. Although up until the end of Abbasid's rule in 1258 CE, Khilafah was in practice, it was gradually turning into monarchy. Both during the times of Ummayads (661-750 CE) and Abbasids (750-1258 CE), Islamic rule expanded beyond Arabia to Egypt, Morocco, Spain, and Portugal in the West, and to the Indian sub-continent in the East. Islamic civilization enriched intellectual life, and Muslim cities became the center of attention for scholars from across the world. However, the element of Monarchy in Islamic governments led to the development of many factors that caused the decline of an ideal Islamic state. The rising tide of Islam took a downward turn through the next few centuries until the colonization of much of the Muslim lands by the European colonial powers.

The history of Islam in America goes as far back as 1717 (Haddad, 1986), when Arabic-speaking slaves were brought by European colonialists from West Africa. Many estimates note that as much as one fifth of the slaves brought into America in the 17th, 18th and early 19th centuries may have been Muslims (Council on Islamic Education, 1994: 18).

About a third of the Muslims in America are African-Americans most of whom recognize Wallac (Warith) Deen Muhammad, son of Elijah Muhammad, founder of the Nation of Islam, as their leader. Warith Deen Muhammad denounced his father's claim of being a messenger of God, and gradually brought his followers in the mainstream Sunni Islam.

Islam in America is the fastest growing religion (AMC: 1994). It has many shades and variations. One of the most challenging tasks the followers of Islam face in America is to be able to use the divine revelation in the context of American pluralism. Islam is capable of addressing change; however Muslims, most of whom have lived for long under oppression either here in America as slaves or in other Muslim countries, have lost the dynamism required for adapting to change under the permanent guidance of God. Muslims' reorganization of their priorities and agendas is a good sign of their progress and strength. This also reflects a better future of Islam in America.

Glossary of Some Important Islamic Terms
A Style Manual

Adhan Call to prayer. A person loudly recites a set of words, prescribed by Muhammd, before each obligatory prayer.

Adl Justice. Establishment of Justice on earth is Islam's primary goal.

Ahl al-bayt People of the House. Refers to the family of the Muhammad. Popularly used to refer to the descendants of the fourth caliph and Muhammad's son-in-law, Ali.

Ahl al-Kitab People of the Book. Refers to Jews, Christians and others who may have received scriptures.

Allah Arabic name of one God. Arabic-speaking Christians and Jews also use this word in the same meaning.

Allahu Akbar God is the greatest. Recited at the beginning of adhan as well as the beginning of every act in prayers.

Amana Divine Trust.

Assalamu Alaikum Peace be upon you. Used upon greeting and leaving a Muslim.

Asr The mid-afternoon prayer. Title of the 103rd chapter of Qur'an. Also means time through the ages.

Ayah Sign or miracle. The term used to refer to a verse of Qur'an.

Ayatullah Sign of God. Title of a high-ranking Shii official.

Baya Oath of allegiance.

Bid'ah an innovation in religion. Deviation from Islamic traditions.

Bismillah In the name of Allah. Used to commence any prayer, action, and recitation of Qur'an.

Black Muslims The term, used to describe the followers of late Elijah Muhammad, is no longer accurate to refer to the African- American Muslims. After his death, the vast majority of African- American Muslims discarded the non-Islamic teachings of Elijah Muhammad and entered mainstream Islam.

Caliph also Khalifah. Successor of Muhammad and leader of Islamic community.

Dar al-harb Abode of war. Non-Islamic territory.

Dar al-Islam Abode of peace. Territory where Islamic law is in force.

Dawah Call or invitation to Islam. Propagation of Islam.

Deen Divine code of life. Religion.

Dhimmi Protected or covenanted people. Non-Muslim citizens of an Islamic State who pay tax (Jizya) in return to the protection and freedom of religion and speech granted to them.

Dua Supplication.

Eid-ul-Adha Feast of sacrifice at the culmination of hajj.

Eid-ul-Fitr Feast of breaking fast marking the end of the month of Ramadan.

Fajr Dawn. First prayer of the day. Name of the 89th Chapter of Qur'an.

Family The foundation of an Islamic society. The peace and stability offered by a stable family unit is greatly valued by Islam. Also considered essential for the spiritual growth of Muslims. Islam considers family to be pivotal in the creation and existence of a harmonious and just social order. The Islamic family does not only consist of parents and children. It is extended to include grandparents, grandchildren, uncles and aunts, etc. Islam has guided the family in its extended form by the laws of dependence and inheritance. It is the obligation of an Islamic family to strengthen the social, cultural, moral, political, and economic fabrics of a society.

Faquih Jurist. One who is an expert of Islamic Jurisprudence.

Faraid Obligations. Also means shares of inheritance prescribed by Qur'an

Fatihah Opening. Name of the First Chapter of Qur'an.

Fatwa a legal religious opinion or decision pronounced by a recognized religious authority, often called a Mufti.

Fiqh Jurisprudence. Religious laws.

Fitnah Confusion, trial, revolt, seduction, discord, riot.

Fundamentalism Not an Islamic term; however, Islamic fundamentalism is widely used to stereotype Muslims. Islam sets out clear guidelines for life. A person who follows these guidelines is simply a devout Muslim.

Ghusl Taking a bath in a religious ceremonial way.

Hadith Narrative report of Muhammad's saying and actions.

Hafiz . One who has memorized the entire Qur'an.

Hajj. Pilgrimage to Makkah on prescribed dates in the 12th Islamic calendar year. Title of the 22nd chapter of Qur'an.

Halal Lawful, legal, permitted by God.

Hanafi School of Islamic jurisprudence founded by Abu Hanifa (d. 767 CE). This school is dominant in many countries that formed part of the Turkish Empire and India.

Hanbali School of Islamic jurisprudence founded by Ahmad ibn Hanbal (d. 855 CE). Dominant in Saudi Arabia and Qatar.

Haram Unlawful. Prohibited by God.

al-Haram The sacred inviolable mosque in Makkah, Saudi Arabia.

Hijab Head covering worn by Muslim women in public

Hijra The Emigration of Muhammad from Makkah to Madinah in 622 CE. Beginning of the first Islamic calendar year.

Ibadat Worship. Religious observances and practices.

Ihram The state entered in order to perform hajj or umrah, the short pilgrimage. Name of the costume that the pilgrims wear.

Ijma Consensus. Agreement of the community. A source of Islamic law.

Ijtihad Independent analysis or interpretation of an Islamic law.

Ilm Knowledge. Science.

Imam Leader. Prayer leader. In Shi'i Islam it refers to the successor of Muhammad and descendent of Caliph Ali. Imam is the political and spiritual leader of Shi'a Muslims.

Insh'allah God willing.

Isha Night prayer, performed about one and a half hours after sunset.

Islah Reform

Islam Peace and submission to the will of God.

Islamic Movement Movement to revive and renew the primacy of the divine guidance sent by God through His prophets, last of whom was Muhammad. Being a dynamic ideology, Islam has a built-in mechanism of renewal, revival, and reform (Qur'an -- 3: 50, 104, 110; 5:48; 7:170; 11:117; 13:38). Islamic movement's main objectives are: 1) To establish Islam as a complete way of life; 2) To integrate individual, social, political, economic, and cultural aspects of life on the basis of Islam; and 3)To restore God's rule in every aspect of life as the supreme source of law.

Islamic movements have always been emerging throughout the history of Islam after Muhammad. Some of the prominent Islamic movements in the last four-to-five hundred years include the efforts lead by Shaikh Ahmad Sirhindi (1564-1624) and Shah Waliullah (1702-1762) in the Indian sub-continent; Muhammad ibn Abd al-Wahab of Makkah, Arabia (1703-1792); Uthman Dan Fodio of Nigeria (1754-1817); Muhammad Ali ibn Al-Sanusi of Libya (1787-1859); Muhammad Ahmad, the Mahdi, of Sudan (1848-1885); Jamal al-Din al-Afghani of Afghanistan and Egypt (1838-1897); Muhammad Abduh (1849-1905) and Rashid Rida (1865-1935) of Egypt; Muhammad Iqbal (1875-1938) and Abul A'la Maudoodi (1903-1979) of the Indian sub-continent; and Hasan al-Banna (1906-1949) of Egypt.

The two major Islamic movements of the Twentieth Century are the Muslim Brotherhood, founded by Hasan al-Banna in Egypt, and the Jamat-e-Islami, founded by Maudoodi in the Indian sub-continent. Both of these movements have influenced Islamic revivalism throughout the world.

The FIS or the Islamic Salvation Front in Algeria, the PAIC or the Popular Arab Islamic Conference in Sudan, the Rifah (now Fazilet)Party in Turkey, The Islamic Party in Malaysia, among others, are organized on the same basic assumption as the Muslim Brotherhood or the Jamaat-e-Islami. However, they differ in their approaches to achieve their objectives. Some are peaceful reform movements, while others consider the use of force as a necessary tool in fighting the enemies of Islam; some are more political than the others.

The Islamic revolution in Iran in 1979 added the revolutionary flavor to the hopes of millions of Muslims throughout the world who were aspiring f or the establishment of the Will of God. However, soon the revolution lost its purity in terms of its universal appeal. Narrow Shii politics dominated the initial call of one Islamic community given by Khomeini.

Whatever one may say about an Islamic movement, it is difficult to deny that its members are the most active players in the revival of Islam as well as the most important element in social reform and economic welfare activities in every place where one finds an Islamic movement. Even those who are involved in armed struggle against repression and tyranny, such as FIS in Algeria and Hamas in Palestine, are known to be the savior of their people.

Unfortunately the media has generalized the term Islamic movement to suit its definition of fundamentalists: people to be condemned; the terrorists; the hard-core Islamists. Such a portrayal of Islamic movement has lead to a gross misunderstanding of an effective movement of our contemporary times.

Jahiliyah The time or period of ignorance. Pre-Islamic Arabia. Also used to refer to an un-Islamic behavior in a society.

Jamaat/Jamaah Congregation. Party.

Jihad Widely miss-quoted to mean holy war. The correct meaning of the word Jihad is struggle, or to strive in the cause of God. It refers to a legitimate struggle against aggression. It is a continuous process of fulfilling God's mission in one's own life and on this earth. Jihad may mean: 1) to struggle for purifying one's own self, to strive to defend Islam, and ultimately to fight against the enemies of God.

Kaaba Cubed-shape building at the Center of the Grand mosque in Makkah. Muslims circle around it and face toward it while praying.

Ka'fir One who rejects the faith. The infidel.

Khalifah Successor of Muhammad. Leader of an Islamic state.

Koran Qur'an. Many non-Muslim writers incorrectly use this spelling for Qur'an (Koran) which is not correct.

Maghrib the sunset prayer.

Maliki School of law founded by Malik Ibn Anas (d. 795 CE). This school is dominant in West Africa and Western Arab countries.

Marriage Contract. A Muslim marriage is not a sacrament, it is a simple legal agreement in which either partner is free to include conditions. Celibacy is condemned and marriage is encouraged. Prearranged marriages have been the prevalent norm among Muslims, though marriages of two individuals committed to each other have always been known and accepted.

Masjid Place of worship, mosque.

Minbar A pulpit in the mosque from where the Imam delivers the sermon on Friday.

Minaret Tower of a mosque. In some mosques the Adhan is given from the minaret.

Mi' raj Ascent. Muhammad's journey to the seven heavens.

Muhammad The last Prophet of Islam (570/571 - 632/633 A. D.).

Mujaddid One who brings about the revival of Islam.

Mujtahid One who is capable of interpreting Islam in new circumstances.

Mumin Believer.

Muslim Name of one who believes in Islam. Moslem is an incorrect spelling of Muslim. In 1990, the Associated Press replaced Moslem by Muslim in its style book.

Muslim and Arab Not every Arab is a Muslim, just as not all Muslims are Arabs. People who speak Arabic as their mother tongue are called Arabs. Besides Muslims there are Christian Arabs and Jewish Arabs.

Muslims, Christian, and Jews Followers of Islam, Christianity and Judaism, the three religions of the Abrahamic order. Muslims consider Christians and Jews as "People of the Book," and recognize their prophets as Prophets of God.

Muezzin One who performs Adhan, the call to daily prayers.

Nation of Islam Currently the followers of Minister Louis Farrakhan. Farrakhan revived Elijah Muhammad's teaching after breaking away from Elijah's son Warith Deen Muhammad in 1978. While many Muslims agree with Farrakhan's message of social and economic upliftment of the black people and their political empowerment, they do not agree and accept his racist approach to religion. "God," said Frrakhan, "is black. God created himself of the material darkness." (Siddiqi, M. 1995: 24). Farrakhan considers Elijah Mohammad as the last prophet. These and many other beliefs and practices are contrary to the teachings of Islam.

Qibla The direction toward Makkah, to which Muslims face when performing prayers.

Qiyas Juristic reasoning by analogy; source of Islamic law.

Riba Usury or Interest. Islam permits increase in capital through trade (Qur'an -- 4:29), and not through lending on usury or interest (Qur'an -- 2:278-279).

Ruku The bow in the canonical prayer, salat.

Sajdah Touching the forehead on the ground during prayer.

Shafi'i School of law founded by Muhammad ibn Idris ash-Shafi'i (d. 820 CE). Followed in Indonesia, Malaysia, Philippines, Egypt, and Central Asia.

Shaytan Satan.

Shi'ism Doctrine of the legitimacy which holds Ali, the fourth Caliph after Muhammad, as the true successor of Muhammad. Emerged during the reign of Yazid, son of the first Ummayad Caliph, Muawiyyah. Shi'as are not members of a sect of Islam; they are Muslims who have different perspectives on certain issues. The major difference lies in the concept of imamate (leadership) instead of caliphate. Beginning from the fourth Caliph, Ali, as the first Imam, all imams have to be descendent of Muhammad. Imam is considered both a political leader and a religious guide. Shi'a Muslims constitute about 10 percent of the total Muslim population.

Shirk Polytheism, idolatry, paganism. Associating others with God.

Shura Consultation. A consultative way of decision making.

Sufi One who gives up all worldly things to seek the pleasure and nearness of God.

Sufism Islamic mysticism.

Sunnah A path, a way of life to be followed. All the traditions and Practices of Muhammad that have become models to be followed by Muslims (Barboza, 1993: 366).

Sunni Muslims who follow the Sunnah of Muhammad. While there is no provision in Islam for labeling groups, the term Sunni is generally applied for the main body of Muslims: over 90 percent.

Tajdid Revival, Renewal.

Talaq pronouncement of divorce or repudiation.

Taqiyya Resort to dissimulation in the face of danger, prevalent among Shi'as.

Taqlid Unquestioned imitation or following.

Tawhid Monotheism. Oneness of God. Absolute sovereignty of God over the Universe.

Ummah Islamic community. A community or nation that transcends ethnic or political definition.

Umrah A pilgrimage to Makkah that can be performed at any time.

Ushr Religious tax on agricultural land.

Vilayt-e-Faqih Guardianship or government by an expert in Islamic law; a Shi'i Islamic concept. One of the highest leadership positions among Shias.

Wahabi Followers of Muhammad ibn Abd al-Wahaab (1703-1787), a Saudi scholar. See themselves as belonging to no school of thought.

Wali Close friend, companion, helper. A religious term used to describe God-loving people.

Waqf Endowment of property for religious purposes.

Women In Islam they are seen as individuals in their own rights. Women are held equal in status and worth. In their religious, ethical and legal rights and obligations, both men and women are equal (Qur'an -- 33:35; 4:124; 16:97; 4:7, 11). A distinct feature of Islam is its emphasis on a dual sex rather than a unisex society. While maintaining the validity of the equal worth of men and women, the Qur'an does not judge this equality to mean equivalence or identity of sexes. Islam assigns both men and women their special responsibilities (Al-Faruqi, L., 1988:39). The division of labor imposes more economic responsibilities on men (Qur'an -- 2:233, 240, 4:34), while women are expected to play a more important role in child bearing and rearing. Islam looks at men and women as complimentary parts of a strong society.

Women are neither inferior to men, nor do they become a rival. They are companions and comrades to each other (Qur'an -- 9:71). Islam presents the model of a family to be patriarchal, putting more burden and responsibility on men and giving them the leadership role within the family (Qur'an 4:34). However, this does not in any way diminishes the opportunities women may have to pursue education, have their own trade or business, and own property. The ultimate aim of an Islamic society is to create mutual love and trust among men and women, and not to make them money-making machines and rivals.

Wudu Ablution, prescribed washing before offering prayers.

Zakat Obligatory prescribed alms to be given by Muslims each year.

Zikr Remembrance of God as an act of worship. Invocation.

Zina Adultery.

Zuhr Noon prayer.
Zulm oppression; sin.

References

Al-Faruqi, Ismail R. and Lois Lamya Al-Faruqi (1986). *The Cultural Atlas of Islam*. New York: Macmillan.

Al-Faruqi, Lois Lamya (1988). *Women, Muslim Society and Islam*. Indianapolis, Indiana: American Trust Publication.

AMC (1994). *Islam & Muslims: An American Style Book*. Washington, D. C.: American Muslim Council.

Athar, Shahid (1993). *25 Most Frequently Asked Questions About Islam*. Indianapolis, Indiana: Shahid Athar.

Barboza, Steven (1994). *American Jihad: Islam After Malcom X*. New York: Doubleday.

Esposito, John L. (1988). *Islam The Straight Path*. New York: Oxford University Press.

Haddad, Yvonne Y. (1986). *A Century of Islam in America*. Occasional Paper No. 4. Washington, D. C.: Islamic Affairs Program, The Middle East Institute.

Husain, Asad and Imran Husain (1996). "A Brief History and Demographics of Muslims in the United States," in Asad Husain, John E. Woods and Javeed Akhtar (eds.) *Muslims in America: Opportunities and Challenges*. Chicago: International Strategy and Policy Institute: 29.

Irving, T. B. (1988). *The Qur'an: Translation and Commentary*. Brattleboro, Vermont: AMANA BOOKS,

Ministry of Information, Saudi Arabia (1994). In the Service of the Guests of God.

Nasr, Seyyed Hossein (1993). *A Young Muslim's Guide to the Modern World*. Chicago: Kazi Publications.

Sardar, Zaiuddin (April 1991). Islam and the Future. *Futures*, Vol. 23, Number 3: 223-230.

Sarwar, Ghulam. *Islam: Beliefs and Teachings*. London, U. K. : The Muslim Educational Trust.

Shaikh, Farzana (ed., 1992). *Islam and Islamic Groups*. New York: Longman, current Affairs.

Siddiqi, Muzammil H. (December 1995). Farrakhan's Islam. *The Message*: 24.

CHAPTER FIVE

Muslims in America
A Summary Profile

Muslims are one of the fastest growing communities in the United States. Their number is estimated to be approximately six million (Husain, 1996). According to an estimate of the American Muslim Council of Washington, D. C. (Council on Islamic Education, 1994) there were six million Muslims in the U. S. in 1993 out of which 42% were African-Americans. (See Table 1 and 2 for details.)

As for Muslims coming to the U. S., some trace their presence in America even before Columbus landed here (Winters, 1977; Mroueh, 1997). Although many would argue against such a finding, most scholars agree that the earliest Muslims in this country arrived from Africa. These were from Morocco, Gambia, and other parts of West Africa. One can find mention of Muslim slaves between sixteenth and nineteenth centuries in historical writings of many scholars. The African- American Muslims in Jamaica, New York, Baltimore, Maryland, and in certain parts of West Virginia and North and South Carolina take pride in being descendants of those early Muslims. Al-Ahari (1989) discusses the presence of a manuscript in Arabic left by an Arabic-speaking Guinean slave, a father of 19 children, who served on a plantation owned by Spalding near Sapelo Island during 1812 and 1855. The earliest known Caucasian American to become Muslim was Alexander Russell Web who became Muslim in the late nineteen century. In his remarkable speech, "The Spirit of Islam," before the first World Parliament of Religion, held in Chicago in 1893, he demonstrated his comprehensive and clear understanding of Islam.

There have been many waves of Muslims coming to the U. S. in the twentieth century. As pointed out by many, including, Haddad (1991), Husain (1996), and Nyang (1992), Muslims from Lebanon, Syria, Yamen, and Turkey were the first to come in the late nineteenth century and during the first quarter of this century. They included mostly Sunnis, but there were many Shiites among them as well. These Muslims settled in larger cities such as Detroit, New York, Los Angeles, and Chicago, as well as in some other industrial areas such as Quincy, Massachusetts, Dearborn, Michigan, and Rochester, New York. Another wave of Muslims' arrival in the U. S. can be traced to

Table 1
Muslim Population in the U. S.

Estimated number of total Muslims in the United States: 6 million*

African Americans = 42.0 %
South Asians = 24.4 %
Arabs = 12.4 %
Africans = 5.2 %
Iranians = 3.6 %
Turkish = 2.4 %
Southeast Asians = 2.0 %
Caucasian Americans = 1.6 %
Undetermined Groups = 5.6 %

* *Introductory Information on Islam and Muslims* by Council on Islamic Education, Fountain Valley, California, 1994: 18.

Table 2

Top Nine Metropolitan Areas Ranked by Friday Prayer Attendance*

City	*Number of Mosques+*	*Number in which Friday prayers are held*	*Average attendance*	*Total attendance*
New York	98	94	292	27,448
S. California	55	49	242	11,858
Chicago	60	58	180	10,440
Washington,DC	31	28	300	8,400
San Fra.By	37	34	203	6,902
N. New Jersey	39	35	181	6,335
Detroit	32	30	183	5,490
Houston	22	21	228	4,788
Philadelphia	25	22	137	3,014

* *Directory of Masjids and Muslim Organizations in North America* (1994). Fountain Valley, California: Islamic Resource Institute: 4

\+ It is estimated that the number of mosques have increased by at least 20% in each of the above cities since the compilation of the above figures. For example, in greater Chicago area there are now more than 75 mosques and places where Friday prayers are held.

immediately after the Second World War. As the political situation in the Middle East changed, large numbers of Palestinians, Syrians, and Egyptians found new homes in America. The next significant influx of Muslims took place after President Lyndon Johnson envisioned the "Great Society" plan. Most immigrants from India, Pakistan, Bangladesh, and Iran came to America during the middle sixties and early seventies. These were mainly students who later found jobs and decided to stay in the U. S. Thus the Muslim community in America reflects the diverse nature of the one billion Muslims who live on this earth. They all believe in one God, in the Qur'an as their book of guidance, and in Muhammad as the last messenger of God; however, they are culturally very different from each other: they speak different languages, and they have different priorities as they assimilate themselves in American society.

Noble Drew Ali's movement of Moorish American Science Temple in 1913 and the Nation of Islam lead by Elijah Muhammad in the early 1930s were primarily socio-political movements created to fight against the injustices done to African-American people and provide them with a sense of identity, respect, and dignity. Elijah Muhammad led a movement of protest and fought against racism and the injustices of the white judicial and political system. In the process he also established a religious and spiritual identity by calling himself "Messenger of Allah" and declaring to be the Imam of the Muslim Community.

The proclamation of being messenger of God put Elijah Muhammad in contradiction with the mainstream Muslims who believe Prophet Muhammad to be the last prophet and messenger of God. However, Elijah Muhammad remained a powerful and dynamic force in uplifting the African-Americans in all aspects of their lives. Elijah gave his people a name, The Nation of Islam, and established mosques, schools, and temples all over the United States. There were more than 60 mosques and centers in 22 states by the year 1960 (Kaba, 1983).

The history of African-American Muslims would be incomplete without mentioning Malcolm X, who became Muslim in early fifties while serving a six year prison term. After his release from prison in 1952, Malcolm X, or Malik El Shabazz, the name Malcolm assumed after performing

Hajj (pilgrimage to the holy city of Makkah or Mecca in Saudi Arabia) in 1964, dedicated his life for the Nation of Islam. He not only increased the number of membership in the Nation from 400 to 40,000 in a few years, but it was due to his dynamic leadership that the Nation of Islam became the focus of attention among Black Americans during the sixties. Many influential African-American personalities entered into the fold of the Nation of Islam due to the efforts made by Malcolm X. These include, among others, Cassius Clay (Muhammad Ali) and Minister Louis Farrakhan. Malcolm streamlined his thoughts, after performing Hajj, and denounced the controversial ideas of Elijah. Malcolm's wife, Betty Shabaaz (1965), describes the change in her husband's thinking and life in these words: "He went to Mecca as a Black Muslim and there he became only a Muslim. He felt that all men were human beings who must be judged on their deeds." However, this created a lot of tension among Elijah's close associates, and resulted in the assassination of Malcolm X on February 21, 1965 in the Audubon Ballroom in New York City.

Macolm has had a profound effect on the way Islam was being preached and practiced among the African-American community in the United States. While clearly recognizing the greater Ummah of Islam, Malcolm was primarily concerned with the plight of Black Muslims and the injustices done to them. This is evident from his answer given to a reporter upon his return from pilgrimage in 1964. When the reporter asked if he would now call himself El-Hajj Malik El-Shahbaaz, Malcolm responded, "Not until the condition of my people changes." (McCloud, 1995)

After the death of Elijah Muhammad on February 25, 1975, Wallac or Warith Deen Muhammad became the leader of the Nation of Islam. Upon assuming leadership, Warith Deen began reconstructing the Nation in two distinct ways: 1) distancing himself and his group from the misleading ways and beliefs of his father, and 2) bringing his people closer to the Qur'an and Sunnah of Prophet Muhammad as well as integrating his people with the rest of the Muslim Community in North America.

Although Warith Deen was able to retain the largest number of followers from among the Nation of Islam, there were many groups that wanted to r etain the teachings of

Elijah in their own distinct ways. The most prominent was the group lead by Minister Louis Farrakhan. Other prominent groups included the one led by Elijah's brother, John Muhammad, in Detroit; Silas Muhammad consolidated his group in Atlanta; Emmanual Muhammad led a small group in Baltimore; and Clarence 13X founded, in New York, a group called "The Five Percenters: The Nation of Gods and Earths."

Most of these groups, however, did not get as much prominence as the group lead by Warith Deen and Farrakhan. While Farrakhan leads a little more than 10,000 followers, his bold initiatives to undo the injustices done to black people and his public criticism of white supremacists and certain Jewish groups have made him the most controversial yet most prominent among the black leaders of America.

Warith Deen, on the other hand, took a gradual and step-by-step approach to build a strong community of more than a million African-American Muslims. He guided his followers away from racial separatism and into a unified Muslim community in North America. Warith Deen Muhammad is also very keen in interfaith efforts and emphasizes upon the need and importance of creating a true understanding of different faiths. In a convention of Jewish and Muslim leaders (*Muslim Journal*: April 14, 1995), Warith Deen strongly urged upon world leaders to build a peaceful world community by respecting the rights of all people of all color, race and religions. "No nation, group or people should seek world dominance, for it will create injustice and oppression, " said Warith Deen. In the early eighties he started the decentralization of his group, and in 1984 declared that the various African-American Muslim communities are no longer centrally bound and local Imams have complete autonomy to lead their groups.

Despite this announcement, Warith Deen continues to enjoy the position of Imam and leader of the largest African-American Muslim group. Beside spiritual guidance, Warith Deen Muhammad also encourages and leads people toward economic, social and political strength with the help of other prominent African American leaders. By strongly supporting the Saudi-American alliance during the Persian Gulf Crisis, Warith Deen established strong ties with the oil-rich kingdom on the one hand, and, on the other, enhanced his group's relationship with the U. S. administration. However, this angered the majority of American Muslims, who were opposed to the U. S. presence in the Gulf, specially in Saudi Arabia. There is no doubt, as observes McCloud (1995, p. 72), " Mr. Muhammad initiated a profound and exceedingly complex process of Islamic growth."

A less known Muslim group is the American-Indian Muslims. Although, not a very organized group, indigenous Americans were reported to be observing Islamic principles even at the time of Columbus (Griggs, 1996), who in his diaries recorded that the Carib Indians of the Islands upon which he landed dressed and performed similar acts of worship as he had seen among the African Muslim Moors. Native Americans came into contact with African Muslim slaves who sought refuge at many of the Indian lands throughout the sixteenth, seventeenth, and eighteenth centuries. Maria Abdin, Umar Ocasio, Abu Aqila Abdullah, Mahir Abdul Razzaq, and Imam Benjamin Perez Mahomat are among the many noted American-Indian Muslim scholars who have documented Muslim communities among the Seminoles, Yaquis, Cherokees, and Choctawas. The history of "social interaction," as writes Griggs (1996), "between African Muslims and Native Americans continued throughout the centuries of trans-Atlantic slave trade as escaped slaves typically found refuge with Indian tribes." Griggs further asserts that, "This history helps to shatter the myth of Indian traditional paganism as the 'foreign' African Muslims seem to have little resistance to their practice and propagation of the way of life of Islam from their host Native Americans."

As for the ideological diversity among the Muslims in America is concerned, there are Sunnis and Shias as well as those who follow various sufi orders. Recently the Naqshbandiya Foundation of America has gained most prominence by organizing annual conferences and celebration of the Prophet's birthday in many parts of the country. However, most Muslims are Sunnis and follow one of the four schools of jurisprudence: the Hanafi, the Shafii, the Maliki, and the Hanbali. Sooner or later, though, there will emerge a jurisprudence that will reflect upon the indigenous trends, needs, and priorities because most Muslims who migrated to America know it very well, as Maher Hathout (1993), a cardiologist by profession who was born in Egypt, says, "we don't consider ourselves to belong to the Middle East or to South Asia. Our roots are there but our present and our future are here."

Many Muslim groups and organizations are deriving inspiration from Islam within the American context. They have their agendas that relate to strengthening the community as well as the country that they now call their home. From politics to family life, and from the activities in the mosques to the political campaigns Muslims are defining their role as part of the American pluralism.

Muslim Organizations and Islamic Centers

The diversity of the Muslim population is well reflected in numerous Muslim organizations serving specific ethnic groups as well as some that claim to be national organizations of Muslims. As mentioned earlier, many organizations were established to serve particular Muslim groups since the beginning of this century; however, among those claiming to be national organizations, Islamic Society of North America (ISNA, established in 1983), Islamic Circle of North America (ICNA, established in 1971), and Muslim American Community under Imam Warith Deen Muhammad (established in 1984 after decentralization of the American Muslim Mission in 1982), are at the forefront of national prominence at this time. Although it lost strength and central leadership after the formation of ISNA in 1983, the Muslim Students Association of U. S. & Canada (MSA), established in 1963, is still a convenient name for Muslim students' activities on university campuses through out the United States and Canada. Except MSA, all the other three organizations mentioned above have several affiliated specialized associations and institutions in addition to their magazines, newspapers, and radio programs. They each attract a particular segment of the Muslim community and provide a social, cultural, and religious forum for their members through annual conventions, regional programs, book services, and elementary and a secondary schools.

One of the earliest Muslim organizations, overshadowed by the emergence of ISNA, ICNA, and others, was established in 1952 by a group of Americans, led, among others, by Abdallah Igram of Cedar Rapids, Iowa. International Muslim Society (IMS) was formed at the end of an Islamic convention held on July 28, 1952 in Cedar Rapids. In the early fifties IMS provided a national forum to Muslims in North America. To accommodate the existing Muslim organizations into this national forum, The Federation of Islamic Associations in the U. S. & Canada (FIA) was established in IMS's third conference, held in Chicago in 1954. FIA was at the forefront of Muslims' activities for about a decade. Even today it has an Islamic Youth Association as an affiliate, an information service, and a 137-acre youth camp in Ohio.

Islamic Society of North America (ISNA) is by far the largest organization of Muslims. Most of ISNA membership comes from immigrants; however, there is a small percentage of African-Americans, Caucasians, and other indigenous Muslims among its membership. ISNA's operational structure consists of its general body, the president, two vice presidents (one each from the United States and Canada), a Majlis Ash-Shura (consultative council), five zonal officers representing three U. S. and two Canadian zones, and many regional representatives. Each zone is divided into three, four or five regions.

The organizational structure of ISNA consists of a central general secretariat, located at ISNA headquarters in Plainfield, Indiana, service institutions, including the North American Islamic Trust (NAIT), the Canadian Islamic Trust (CIT), Islamic Book Service (IBS), and Islamic Teaching Center (ITC), specialized organizations including the Muslim Students Association of the U. S. & Canada (MSA), Muslim Communities' Association (MCA), and Muslim Youth Association (MYNA), and professional associations including the Association of Muslim Social Scientists (AMSS), Association of Muslim Scientists and Engineers (AMSE), and Islamic Medical Association (IMA). ISNA publishes a bi-monthly magazine, *Islamic Horizon*, whose circulation has reached over 50,000 (Islamic Horizon, January/February 1997: 15). Although it experienced many challenges, including financial difficulties, ISNA has been able to survive and provide Muslims a general, social, cultural, and religious forum. Some of its recent efforts include launching of a television network, ISNA Vision, community leadership and management programs, and summer internship and training for students and Imams. ISNA Vision is still in its very rudimentary stage. ISNA's main shortcomings are its lack of dynamic leadership, a failure to attract significant number of indigenous population among its rank and file, and lack of focused programs and events. Nonetheless, in less than fifteen years ISNA has been at the forefront of Muslims' collective presence in North America.

Islamic Circle of North America (ICNA) was founded in 1971 by a number of MSA members who wanted to launch an Islamic movement in North America. This is evident from their goal as it is stated in ICNA By-Laws (1994): "The goal of ICNA shall be to seek the pleasure of Allah (SWT) through the struggle of Iqamat-ud-Deen (establishment of the Islamic system of life) as spelled out in the Quran and the Sunnah of Prophet Muhammad (SAW)." The various activities of ICNA include the Sound Vision, a multimedia company producing video, audio, and computer programs especially for children and young adults; MSI Financial Corporation, an interest-free investment and financing institution; *The Message*, a monthly news magazine with over 20,000 circulation; *Young Muslim*, a recently started magazine for young Muslims; Muslim Alert Network, a media monitoring organization; ICNA Book Service; ICNA Relief, a world wide relief agency; Neighbor net, a community organization for developing a strong family and neighborhood; and a network of Islamic propagation center. ICNA is trying to evolve itself as a major North American Islamic organization, although its membership is still predominantly immigrants from Pakistan and India. It is still to be seen whether ICNA can detach itself from the back-home links and priorities.

The Muslim American Community, under the leadership of Imam W. Deen Muhammad, has gone through several major changes since Imam W. Deen took over its leadership in 1975. Imam W. Deen has recently assumed a new title as the "Muslim American Spokesman." He commands the largest group of Muslims in North America, over a million African-American Muslims. His lectures are available in audio tapes, booklets, over a nationwide network of radio programs, and through an on-line website. The *Muslim Journal* is a weekly newspaper with a circulation of more than 100,000 reaching about a million people. Imam W. Deen also guides a nationwide network of elementary and secondary schools under the "Sister Clara Mohammad School" system. Many activities, including an annual convention, youth workshops, educational conferences, and Imam training workshops have now become regular features of Imam W. Deen Muhammad's efforts to mobilize the African-American Muslims in North America. All of these activities are conducted under the supervision of the Ministry of Imam W. Deen Mohammed.

In addition to the above there are scores of Muslim organizations that are working for a diversity of Islamic and Muslim causes to serve different groups of Muslims. Some of the Islamic Centers in major metropolitan areas such as Chicago, Los Angeles, and New York may also be treated as significant Muslim organizations because each of them has a very large membership, sometimes even larger than many so-called national organizations. For example, the Muslim community Center, the Islamic Foundation, and the Mosque Foundation in the greater Chicago area cater to the needs of more than 1000 members each, have their own weekend schools, grade and secondary schools, bookstores, and monthly publications. The Islamic Center of Southern California has a membership of more than 2000, publishes a monthly magazine, *The Minaret*, with over 15000 circulation, operates a major bookstore and a large elementary school, and has a political affiliate body, the Muslim Public Affairs Council (MPAC) that functions both within the state and at Capitol Hill as a lobbying group educating and lobbying for issues of concern to the Muslim community in North America. There are more than twenty similar Islamic Centers nationwide that function like a comprehensive Muslim organization, and not merely as a community center.

According to a survey conducted by the Islamic Resource Institute (1994, p. 3), there are 1, 046 mosques and Islamic centers in the U. S., about 22 percent of which is owned and operated by Muslim students at college and university campuses nationwide. However, Ghazi (1995) has quoted Koszegi (1992), who has catalogued 1, 227 mosques and Muslim centers in the U. S. Ghazi further observes that, "In the last three years, since the above list [by Koszegi] was prepared, the number of mosques and centers has grown enormously." In the directory prepared by the Islamic Resource Institute, the top nine cities with the largest number of mosques are: 1) New York, 2)Southern California (Los Angeles and Vicinity), 3) Chicago, 4) Washington, D. C., 5) San Francisco Bay area, 6) North New Jersey, 7)Detroit, 8)Houston, and 9) Philadelphia. (see Table 1). Appendix I lists the major Muslim organizations in the U.S. , whereas Appendix L provides a listing of major Islamic Centers in areas of significant Muslim population in the U. S.

In addition to the Islamic organizations mentioned above, there are many professional associations serving the specific needs of Muslim professionals. These associations and institutions hold conferences, seminars, and workshops; publish journals, periodicals, and monographs; give scholarship to students; and encourage Muslims to utilize their professional skills in articulating the principles of Islam in such a manner that they can become more efficient and productive in serving the Muslims in America in particular, and the community at large in general. Some of these associations and organizations, such as the Council of American Islamic Relations (CAIR) and the American Muslim Council (AMC), have attracted the attention of Muslims and non-Muslims alike in recent years due to the significant success in their respective areas of activities, i. e. media monitoring and media relations and lobbying and political networking to benefit Muslims. In February, 1992, a group of Muslim professionals and academicians established the North American Associations of Muslim Professionals and Scholars (NAAMPS). Since its inception NAAMPS has been emphasizing issues and agendas that are relevant to the development and growth of Muslims in North America. Some of the unique features of NAAMPS are its well focused conferences, its emphasis on changing the status-quo, and its effort to promote free thinking among Muslim professionals. (See Appendix J for a list of Muslim Professional organizations.)

Another category of specialized organizations are the business and professional service organizations ranging from bookstores and financial institutions to Muslim web sites and media outlets. A list of such major organizations is provided in Appendix H.

It seems that Muslims are entering into a new phase of their existence in this country. After spending much of the latter half of this century catering to the community's internal needs, Muslims are now looking outward. They are dealing with media and with political institutions. They are now making a lot of efforts into developing mutually beneficial relationships with the American people at large. During the past several years Muslims have contributed significantly in interfaith dialogues and interfaith relationships. Their outlook and vision is now based on a more proactive rather than reactive approach. They are establishing think tanks, financial institutions, publishing houses, political action committees, and educational and research institutions. As Haddad (1994) has noted, "It is perhaps inevitable that Muslim Communities in America to some degree will adapt, accommodate, and acculturate to the realities of existence in the American context. . . . Muslims are, in fact, both understanding of the need for this kind of adaptation and creative in finding ways in which to make it happen while still remaining true to their understanding of what it means to be Muslim."

It seems certain that despite the negative media portrayal and efforts by some vested interests to keep on creating stereotypes about them, they are going to be as much a part of American mosaic as any other well established community is when the twenty-first century dawns in America.

References

Al-Ahari, Muhammad Abdullah (Spring, 1989). "Bilali: They Say He was a Slave. Yes He was. But a Slave of God," *The Minaret*: 26.

Council on Islamic Education (1994). *Introductory Information on Islam and Muslims*. Fountain Valley, California: Council on Islamic Education: 18.

Ghazi, Abidullah Ansari and Khwaja Moinul Hassan (1995). "A Brief History of Islam in the United States," unpublished manuscript: 49.

Griggs, Khalid Abdul Fattah (July 1996). "On the Good Red Path," *The Message*, v. 21 (#1): 6.

Haddad, Yvonne Yazbeck (1991). *The Muslims of America*. New York: Oxford University Press.

Haddad, Yvonne Yezbeck and Jane Idleman Smith [eds.] (1994). *Muslim Communities in North America*. Albany, New York: State University of New York Press: xxix.

Hathout, Maher (May 2, 1993). As quoted in *The New York Times*: 1.

Husain Asad and Imran Husain (1996). "A Brief History and Demographics of Muslims in the United States," in Asad Husain, John E. Woods and Javeed Akhtar (eds.) *Muslims in America: Opportunities and Challenges*. Chicago: International Strategy and Policy Institute: 29.

ICNA By-Laws (1994). *The Charter and By-Laws*. Jamaica, New York: Islamic Circle of North America: 3.

Kaba, Lansine (1983). "Today, Islam, Which Has Been in Existence Four Centuries, Is Growing Dramatically: Through the 'Black Muslim' Experience, Many Americans Have Discovered Islam," *Afrique History U. S.* v. 1 (#4):33-37, as quoted in Michael A. Koszegi and J. Gordon Melton [eds.] (1992). *Islam in North America: A Source Book*. New York: Garlend Publishing.

McCloud, Aminah Beverly (1995). *African American Islam*. New York: Routledge: 37.

Mroueh, Youssef (July, 1997). "Pre-Columbian Muslims in the Americas," *The Message*: 17-19.

Nyang, Sulayman S. (1992). "Islam in the United States of America: A Review of the Sources," in Michael A. Koszegi and J. Gordon Melton (eds.). op. cit. : 3-24.

Shabaaz, Betty (1965). As quoted in the *Pittsburgh Courier*, March 6, 1965: 4.

Winters, Clyde-Ahmad (1977). "Islam in Early North and South America," *Al-Ittihad*, July-October: 57-61.

CHAPTER SIX

Media and Muslims
Mutually Beneficial Relationship

There is nothing mystical in the dawning of a century. The sun will still rise in the East and set in the West. The seasons will still merge with one another. But human beings have always used the milestones of time to ponder the past and peer into the future. There is no doubt that the dawning of the 21st century marks the first time the Muslim community in North America enters an era so conscious of itself, so serious about evaluating its deep-rooted legacy, and so deliberate about its direction.

In their effort to build a strong Muslim community in the U. S., Muslims have, for long, overlooked or underestimated the role and power of media in shaping and molding American public opinion. At the same time, media have also treated Muslims as a weak minority with a religion that was mostly seen and understood in the context of various international conflicts. However, there have been significant improvements at both ends. Muslims are becoming more skilled and organized in dealing with media. Their focus is shifting from complaints to media monitoring and media relations. Media too are realizing the need to present a more realistic image of one of the fastest growing communities in the U. S. At this juncture it is important that both the media and Muslims realize the need for establishing a common ground or a mutually beneficial relationship between them. This requires that both understand how to serve each other's needs and satisfy concerns. Whereas media must do away with Islam and Muslim bashing and rely on sources that have credibility with both the Muslims and the media, Muslims must also become more active and increase their interaction with media as well as the general American publics. This chapter provides some general guidelines for both the Muslims and the American media to engage in a proactive and constructive relationship with one another.

Muslims and Media

There are many steps Muslims can take for shaping a better relationship with media:

1. Understanding media structure, power, practices, politics, and media economics.

2. Learning what media consider newsworthy, and communicating community events and actions that fit the definition of news worthiness.
3. Providing the media with easy access to Muslim's informed view-points.
4. Taking responsibility for correcting misinformation about Islam and Muslims.
5. Committing greater financial resources to the training of media resource persons among Muslims, to the establishment of media relations offices, and to the establishment of effective media outlets owned and operated by Muslims.

Understanding Mass Media

Contemporary mass media have emerged along with the emergence of the modern nation-states and with those of the contemporary ideologies. On the one hand, media reflect the interest and perspectives of the dominant groups, and on the other, they also embody, in their practices, the notion of separation of church and state. Muslims must know that the American media, in general by their nature, look at religion and religious activities with distrust, secular bias, and indifference. Dart and Allen (1994), in analyzing the coverage of religion and the communities of faith, conclude that, "Secular journalism and sacred religion suspiciously eye one another. Their traditional perspectives and goals are at odds."

The new information technologies are rapidly changing the shape of American media. Web sites and on-line technology have given a new meaning to media. Most of the major newspapers, magazines, and television networks now have their own web sites in which the contents are readily available to the media consumers. Cable networks are challenging the traditional networks and forcing them into mergers. The mega merger of Turner's cable empire with Time-Warner has created the largest media conglomerate. Only about 15 conglomerates own most of the print and broadcast media networks. When a handful of people control what reaches more than 260 million Americans, fairness, objectivity and freedom of speech of individual citizens are being threatened. In such circumstances, it is easy for the media to indulge in stereotyping and dehumanizing of a particular group if for some reason they wish to do so.

For the most part Muslims are concerned with the news media, the basic task of which is to report facts: events that are considered newsworthy by the media themselves. Usually the news worthiness is determined on the basis of an event's impact, its closeness and appropriateness to the local readers/viewers (proximity), the prominence of the people who are in the story or part of the event to the readers/viewers, and the timeliness -- how soon the event is reported or conveyed to the media? Another factor that sometime dominates over most of the above is the element of conflict, crime, and disaster. It is easier to sell a story if it has a sensational value. Even most serious of the media reporting adheres to this notion. That is why most of the times newspapers, magazines, radio, and television ignore many important events or hard news over a scandal in which a prominent person is involved or a story in which conflict and crime is at the core. No matter how much we dislike conflict in the news, it is we the people who have been for long giving such shows top ratings.

What should Muslims do?

The bottom line for Muslims is to ask the question: how news worthy is that which media reports? News worthiness should always be evaluated from the media's point of view, and not only from a Muslim's perspectives.

Any individual, group, or organization intending to deal with media should develop a media strategy and a media plan. Muslims are responsible for what is said about Islam and themselves in media. News about Islam and Muslims will not just happen, Muslims have to make an effort to make it happen. In this regard the following simple points may be helpful.

Never, Never have no comments. There is no excuse for not having a response on an important issue that concerns Muslims locally, nationally, or internationally or even on an issue of general concern on which there should be a Muslim response. When a reporter calls, one may not be prepared instantaneously to respond. It is o.k. to ask the reporter when is the deadline and then call back with a proper explanation. It is better than having lost the opportunity to respond.

Getting the media excited about a story. There are a number of tests to determine how excited or interested the media may be in a story having a Muslim perspective.

a. Is it news? Just because the Muslims think it's pretty remarkable is not a guarantee that media will also care about the story.

b. To whom? The broader the impact of the story/event, the greater the opportunities for media coverage. If something affects Muslims only and had no or very little relevance for the general readers/viewers, why should media care? One should think about enlarging the impact by showing how something that has happened within the Muslim community can be of interest or can benefit or be of relevance to larger audiences.

c. What will work best? Determining what will work best in a particular situation is a key to success. If one is not sure , one should write a pitch letter to find out if a particular journalist will be interested in a story or will be interested to cover a particular event at a Muslim center. A pitch letter is a simple one-page letter inquiring about the acceptability of a story or a topic on which one wishes to write. The media can be influenced by pitching a story idea or by inviting a reporter to a special event organized by Muslims. It is always better to take initiative than to wait for the media to call.

A media advisory is another useful way to generate interest among the journalists about an event that is planned for Muslims. Sometimes a feature story is the best piece of writing, and at other times a news release works better. Which one will be best to use in a particular situation is the job of the person who is responsible for media relations on behalf of a particular Muslim community.

Building long-term media relations and becoming a news resource. A proactive and long-term relationship with the media is the most effective way of getting most out of the media. The relationship must be one of mutual trust and mutual advantage. The person or persons responsible for this should have the full confidence of their organizations and of the media. This is not usually so easy. Often the interests of the organization and those of the media are at odds. Organizations want news reported in a favorable manner that will portray a positive image; the news media want news that will interest readers and viewers. Both objectives appear to be natural. The job of those trying to establish a mutually beneficial relationship with media is to develop and work on a strategy that satisfies both ends. Some of the basic principles (Cutlip, 1997) for establishing good media relations are the following.

1. Shoot squarely.
2. Give service.
3. Don't beg or carp.
4. Don't ask for kills.
5. Don't flood the media.
6. Keep updated lists.

Shoot squarely means being accurate, candid, honest, and skillful. Providing factual information with supporting documents in a format that is acceptable to the media opens the door of persuasion. Dealing professionally enhances the chance of winning over.

Give service. The quickest and surest way to gain the cooperation of media practitioners is to provide them with interesting, timely stories and pictures that they want and in the form in which they can readily use the stories. One should not simply be a news source; instead one should be a media resource. News is a highly perishable commodity and it occurs round the clock. Media practitioners lean on and cooperate with those who are willing to respond to a midnight call for a picture of an organization's president and a story about the burning of a mosque. A readily available media kit is often appreciated by journalists.

Don't beg or carp. If a story is not sufficiently newsworthy, begging or carping will not help it get published or broadcasted. It will annoy and irritate the journalists who hold their jobs by knowing what interests people. Too many people lose the trust and confidence of the media by trying to become editors themselves. They refuse to acknowledge that determining and selecting what is news is the job of a media practitioner.

Don't ask for kills. No matter how frank one is with an editor or reporter, one should never ask to suppress or kill another story in order to accommodate his/her own story. It is very unprofessional and unethical to ask for kills. It only reflects upon one's own poor taste and bad judgment. The media, none the less, will do their job and report what is worthy of reporting.

Don't flood the media. Too much publicity is bad publicity. Simply sending a press release to 500 media outlets and sending it too frequently do not ensure that it will be published. One should use good judgment about what is being sent to media, when it should be sent, to whom it should be sent (which media outlet or outlets are most appropriate), how it should be sent (what is the most appropriate format to get media attention. Is it a press release, a feature story, a media advisory, or a media kit?), and why it should be sent (what objectives are to be achieved?). Careful analysis and answers of these questions will help determine the appropriateness of media usage.

Keeping updated lists. A generic message often gets lost. Few things could be more annoying to an editor than to receive a press release or a feature article addressed to the person who has been replaced two or three years earlier. Keeping an updated mailing list helps address material to the person who is responsible to cover community news or religious features. This also shows one's knowledge of the media outlets and people who work there.

In conclusion, long term media relations should be based on honesty, speed, brevity, and confidence. One should be as frank and cooperative in giving bad news as in giving good news. Good media relations require accepting, without any reservation, the fact that media has to serve the people's right to know and whatever may be happening around them. Good media relations are not bestowed, they are earned. Long term and profitable media relations can also be established by adhering to the five "Fs, " which means dealing with media in a manner that is fast, frank, factual, fair, and friendly.

Media contact strategy. Media contacts are a combination of mailing/e-mailing and follow-up phone calls. When contacting reporters, editors or broadcasters about an event or a story, one should know what he/she is going to say to sell his/her idea in thirty seconds or less. If one is not sure what the news element of the story/event is, one won't be effective in selling it. The ability to effectively and convincingly educate a reporter to the value of one's story or story angle is tough. But it is the difference between media relations and media notification, the difference between media relations and no media attention.

National vs. local media attention. National media attention usually means the weekly news magazines, *The New York Times*, *Wall Street Journal*, *USA Today*, network television and radio programs. The window of opportunity for national media attention is highly sought and very limited in space and/or time. Unless there is really an issue/event of national importance, one should try the local and regional media. One can reach more people and influence just as effectively and more efficiently through the local and regional media.

Generating News. There are many ways Muslims can attract media attention. Special events such as beginning and/or end of Ramadan, Eid-ul-Fitr, Eid-ul-Adha, and Juma prayers, and local Muslims going or returning from pilgrimage to Makkah (Hajj) are but a few examples. Inauguration of a new mosque, Islamic school, lecture by a prominent Muslim scholar, protest rallies on a local, national and/or international issue of concern, and recognition and/or fund raising dinners may also be used to generate news in order to attract media attention. In all of the above cases one or more of the media tools such as a media advisory, a press release, and/or a news conference may be used to reach the media. (For samples of these materials see appendix A - D).

As a general guideline one should remember to incorporate the criteria of news worthiness into special events. This can be done in many ways. For example, to give prominence to a rally in support of Palestine, Bosnia, or Cosovo, it can be tied in with a security council meeting on the issue or a vote in the United Nations, or by inviting a prominent person, such as a senator, a member of the Congress, or a prominent person from any of these regions, to address the rally. The local angle is always sought by local media. Creating or emphasizing the local angle concerning a special event is another way news worthiness can be increased.

Visuals attract media attention whether print or broadcast, and increase the value of an event from media's perspective. It is important to point out in a press release or media advisory if there will be a photo opportunity or an event that may provide good video footage.

Important consideration should also be given to the timing of events. Afternoons are usually the worst time to invite a reporter, especially a broadcast crew. The best time is usually between 10:00 a.m. and 1:00 p.m. or between 7:00 and 9:00 p.m. in the evening.

Being accessible to the media. Muslims and especially their leaders should be available and accessible to the media. There is a need for an informed point of view from an Islamic/Muslim perspective, and it is the responsibility of Muslim leaders to provide that. In order to be more effective, there should be a short course or workshop designed to make media-trained and media-literate any Muslim who assumes leadership in the Muslim community. Islamic centers should have articles, readily available for media use, on Islam, Islamic festivals, Islamic positions on various social, cultural, national and international issues, and about the local Muslim community and its leadership. Many international issues need well-thought-out Muslim points of view. Instead of reacting to a wrongly stated position in the media, Muslims should take initiative and present their own point of view without any delay. Some times no response may be a good response, but this should be decided upon by Muslim leadership.

Another important point at the core of accessibility issue is our understanding that Muslims and Americans live in two different worlds, one surrounded by the high walls of Islamic shariah and the other a vast, barren immoral world. This point can be well understood if one listens to the tapes of speeches made at Muslim conventions and read what is written in the newsletters published by most Islamic centers and in many Muslim-owned magazines. If as a Muslim one is reluctant to hand over such materials to a fellow American, a media practitioner or a neighbor, one should be more sensible in his/her speeches and publications.

Media interviews and talk shows. An important opportunity to utilize the media for presenting the Muslim point of view is through interviews and talk shows (Hooper, 1993). Local newspapers and magazines may be interested or may be made interested in presenting the Muslim point of view on various issues that are important for the local media consumers. There are local or syndicated talk show programs on radio and television that may provide an opportunity to present the Muslim perspective. In certain cases Muslims may be invited to participate in a talk show or may be requested for an interview; however, in some other situation one may have to seek for an opportunity to get interviewed or to get invited on a talk show. In either case, the best way to get ready for an interview is to consider the following.

1. Have clear answers for the 5 W's and an H...variations on what, when, where, who, why and how questions.

2. Before appearing for an interview one must get enough preparation and have at least two rehearsals.

3. One should develop a list of three or four important thoughts that one intends the reporter to be able to capture during the interview.

4. One should have a thorough knowledge of the audience as well as the medium. Every medium has certain advantages and certain disadvantages over the others. Newspaper reporters have to meet deadlines on a daily basis, so they may need answers instantly. Magazine articles, in most cases, are prepared much ahead of publication dates, so there is opportunity for delaying the response if one needs time to research and find out certain information. Each magazine caters to a very specialized audience, and, except the news magazines, the news hole

(space for news) in most magazines is very limited. So the responses in a magazine interview need to be more specific to the concerns and needs of the particular audience that the magazine serves. For both the newspaper and magazine one should never say something that he or she does not want to see in print. This is also true for radio and television interviews. There is nothing off the record. If you don't want to be quoted, simply don't say it.

In radio the answers and the way of delivery need to be sharp, crisp, and to the point. Radio listeners will only listen to words once, so they must be uttered clearly and in good pace. Use of jargons and multiple syllable-words should be avoided as much as possible.

Television interviews or talk shows, live or taped, are the toughest media work that require much more preparation and several rehearsals. They are tough because there is a lot more to keep under control, but a picture is worth a thousand words.

One should know the difference between a television interview in one's own office or center and in a television studio, as well as the difference between a live television interview and a taped one. If doing an interview in one's office, one should pre-select a setting with which he or she is comfortable and which is attractive but not cluttered. The setting should also reflect the character and nature of one's organization. If the interview is in a television studio, one should always arrive at the studio with lots of time to spare so that he or she may get familiar with people (technicians as well as the host) and the environment. Following are some helpful tips for a successful television interview or a talk show appearance (Silk, 1990).

1. Knowing the program audience and the interviewer or the show's host and his or her interviewing techniques and biases if any.

2. Finding out how the host would like to be referred to.

3. Getting relaxed and comfortable.

4. Dressing appropriately. Neither being too formal nor too informal.

5. Ignoring the technical equipment around and concentrating on the host, audience and the topic of the interview/talk show.

6. Feeling what one is saying will make one comfortable with the host and the audience. One should always try to make eye contact with the host and the camera, and have a smiling face even when answering the toughest question or dealing with a very difficult or controversial subject.

7. Being prepared, assertive, and polite are the three cardinal rules for making a point effectively. Arguing with the host or the other participant of a talk show should be avoided as much as possible. Even if the host or another participant in the talk show makes a negative comment, one should never repeat it. Instead, one should positively answer the question. A direct question should be answered in a direct way. One should listen to the question carefully and be articulate in the answer. There is no harm in saying, "I don't have an answer at this time." It is better than guessing or messing up the question.

8. Remember the three best secrets to the successful performance on a television interview or talk show: practice; practice; and practice.

A long-term strategy. It is important that more financial resources are committed to the development of print, audio and video materials that can be used by Muslims locally to interact with media. It is also important that Muslims are trained in some of the above skills necessary for mutually beneficial media relations. This requires media workshops and seminars, not just once and at one place, but on a continuous basis and in every place with significant Muslim presence. Each local Muslim/Islamic center should have a media relations committee consisting of five to six persons who are well trained in various media skills. A few of these should serve as Muslim spokes-persons who could effectively present Muslim/Islamic points of view on a radio or television talk show.

North American cities with major Muslim population such as Chicago, New York, Los Angeles, San Francisco, Detroit, Houston, Cleveland, Dallas, Miami, Toronto, and Montreal should have regional media committees and media training centers.

On the national level there is a need for a mass media institute of training and research. This can serve as 1)a feeding ground for an ongoing effort to produce high quality print and broadcast material for Muslim as well as media usage; 2)a center to prepare media resource persons, spokes-persons, and trainers; 3)a research center to gather data and information that can be used by Muslims nationwide to deal with media as well as policy makers; and 4) a center for the development of Muslim-owned print and broadcast media that can serve as effective mass media channels to reach North American Muslims and fellow Americans at large.

The above needs a non-partisan approach by Muslims, an approach that is above organizational politics. Media are expensive. Unless Muslims pool their resources, they will not be able to produce effective print and broadcast mass media of their own. For several years a number of national Muslim organizations have been trying to establish their own national radio and television networks without success. Obviously, the lack of both the human and material resources is a big hurdle.

CARE is the only effective Muslim media monitoring agency in North America; however, its scope is very limited. What CARE is doing in one area, Muslims need to effectively do in many of the above described areas.

Beyond media relations, media monitoring and media training, is the issue of change in attitude. Muslim parents and young Muslims should realize the significance of Muslim media graduates. Muslims investment in this area is insignificant. Compared to Muslims with medical, engineering, computer science, business management, and law degrees, Muslims with a journalism degree are fewer than half a percent. There is no substitute for a strong Muslim presence in the American media establishments, both print and broadcast. Muslim stereotyping will more quickly disappear if there are Muslims on the staffs of newspapers, magazines and broadcast media.

The proactive approach to media emphasizes multi-dimensional and on going efforts, some of which have been illustrated above. While there is a certain element of deliberate mischief and conspiracy, living continuously under the conspiracy theory is very detrimental to healthy growth.

Media's responsibility.

So far the author has discussed what Muslims should do to establish mutually beneficial relationships with media. Now here are a few words about what media ought to do to better their coverage of Islam and Muslims.

Learning more about Islam from Islamic sources. A lot has been written about Islam by non-Muslim authors. Some of it may be accurate and fair, but some of it may not be. Today there is hardly a major North American city without a significant Muslim population and major Islamic Centers. Media practitioners should refer to these centers (See addresses in the appendix) for expert opinions when writing on issues involving Muslims and Islam. Media practitioners need to understand the nature of cultural, social, and religious diversity within the Muslim community in the united States in particular and the world in general.

Religion-beat reporters, writers, and broadcasters need fellowships and seminars (Dart and Allen, 1993) to give depth to religion coverage. Muslim spokes persons and media liaison persons may be invited to such seminars and workshops. Many surveys have shown that religion writers land in their jobs most of the time by chance and have no previous knowledge of a particular religion, especially Islam.

Use of appropriate terminology and words. For long media have used pejorative and inflammatory words and terminologies such as Moslems instead of Muslims, Mohammedans referring to followers of Islam, fundamentalism, nomadic, barbaric, uncivilized, anti-modern etc. The best would be to use terms that are used by Muslims themselves. Refer to chapter four for a short glossary of Islamic terms.

Doing away with unexamined and hidden assumptions. Many times media seem to follow or support the status-quo. Several studies, including those of Said (1981) and Mowlana (1992), have documented how many of the media reports about the Iranian revolution, about the Persian Gulf War, about Saddam's accumulation of weapons of mass destruction, and about the so-called Muslim fundamentalists in Algeria were more a triumph of media imagery than an objective analysis of the situation or a piece of information/news based on hard facts and data. Several examples in chapters two and three document this fact that this helps more in stereotyping Muslims and Islam than serving the "people's right to know." Media practitioners ought to be as demanding in scrutinizing reports involving Muslims and Islam as they are in other cases in which the reports are based on unquestionable facts rather than hidden assumptions.

Minimum use of religious labels. In a comparative study (MPAC, 1995), it was found that when religion was an apparent motivating factor for violent incidents, religious labels were used 50 percent of the time for stories involving Muslims, 10 percent of the times involving Jews, and a negligible amount involving Christians. At the very least, Muslims hope to put an end to preferential treatment in the media. At best, Muslims would like to see all religious labels dropped.

Some of the recommendations made by Dart and Allen (1994) in *Bridging the Gap: Religion and the News Media*, are also true in reporting Islam and Muslims. With some modifications these are:

1. Islam should be recognized as a fascinating, news-laden subject for coverage that resonates with the fastest growing community in the US, the Muslims.

2. Television should seek inventive ways to handle news about Muslims and Islam in America.

3. Covering Islam and Muslims should be a regular news beat in major metropolitan cities in the U. S. where the Muslim population is 100,000 or more.

4. Small town newspapers and radio should approach the coverage of Islam and Muslims creatively. In many rural and small communities newspapers and radio cover Islam only when it is reported in major media in the context of a major violence involving Muslims and non

Muslims. Many of these community and small town media do cover religion positively and creatively; they only have to include positive coverage of Islam and Muslims on a more frequent basis.

The author would like to end this book with the hope that the dawning of the twenty-first century will mark the beginning of a fiduciary relationship between media and Muslims in the United States, and that it will end the suspicion at both ends. Islam, in its broadest sense, is the religion of universal peace. It aspires to create a society free of all types of biases, hatred, and prejudices. It cherishes truth, progress, civility, openness, diversity, and fair play. Media, in its ideal form, is an instrument to capture events in their right context as they unfold. In the true sense, the job of a media practitioner is to serve, in an unhampered way, the people's right to know without attempting to color people's knowledge or give it a particular meaning or angle.

If Muslims can uphold and embody the spirit of Islam and the practitioners of media can adhere to the "Canons of Journalism, " the mutually beneficial relationship will not be difficult to establish and maintain.

References

Cutlip, Scott, Allen H. Center and Glen M. Broom (1994). *Effective Public Relations* (7th ed.). Englewood Cliffs, N. J.: Prentice-Hall: 305.

Dart, John and Jimmy Allen (1994). *Bridging the Gap: Religion and the News Media.* Nashville: The Freedom Forum First Amendment Center at Vanderbilt University: 59-64.

Hooper, Ibrahim (1993). *How to Influence the Mass Media: A Handbook for Muslim Activists.* Minneapolis, Minnesota: The Islamic Information Service.

Mowlana, Hamid, George Gerbner, and Herbert I. Schiller (eds.) (1992). *Triumph of the Image: The Media's War in the Persian Gulf-- A Global Perspective.* Boulder, Colorado: Westview: 6.

MPAC (1995). "Religious Labels and the Rabin Assassination: A Survey of Three major U. S. Newspapers," (Occasional Paper). Los Angeles: Muslim Public Affairs Council: 5.

Said, Edward (1981). *Covering Islam: How the Media and the Experts Determine How We See the Rest of the World.* New York: Pantheon: 104.

Silk, Susan L. (1990). *Media Training Guide*. Chicago: Media Strategy Training Center: 55.

Appendixes

Appendixes

A. Press Release

B. Media Advisory, Pitch Letters, and Letter to the Editor

C. Media Kit

D. News Conference and Special Events

E. Examples of Good Media coverage

F. National Broadcast Media Directory

G. National News Magazines and Major Newspapers with Full Time Religion Writers/Editors

H. Muslim Media Directory

I. Muslim Financial Institutions

J. Muslim Organizations

K. Muslim Professional Associations, Research Institutes, and Political Organizations

L. Muslim Service Organizations, Bookstores, and Publishers

M. Directory of Islamic Centers

Appendix A

Press Release

A press release, also known as a news release, is the most common format for generating news and publicity for an organization. About 60 percent of the editorial contents of *The New York Times* and *Washington Post* are generated through press releases and other publicity material received by these papers (Aronson, 1993). However, the competition is extremely tough and only a few of the thousands of press releases are used by the media.

The main function of a press release is to announce a newsworthy event in an organization, to introduce new officials, to announce new services offered by an organization, and sometimes to counter bad publicity in crisis situations.

The most important aspect of a press release is its news worthiness, which is determined in terms of the five W's and an H questions, all of which are briefly answered in the first paragraph known as the lead. Example: (Who ?) Renowned Muslim Scholar Azhar Shariff (What?) will visit (Where?) Chicago's Muslim Community Center (When?) Sunday , June 14, 1998, at 10:00 a.m. (Why?) to inaugurate the full time secondary school for Muslim girls. (How?) Dr. Shariff will preside over the inauguration and deliver the keynote speech.

Each release must be tailored for its medium in order to be in the competition for being picked up by an editor. Usually the release should be in a news story format for a newspaper; a little longer feature style for magazines, trade and business publications; terse, radio-style release for radios; and television news scripts with visuals for television station. Sending a photograph along with a news story type release to a radio station is of no avail.

Sending the release to the right person is another important point to remember. One must know the behind-the-scene peoples, the gatekeepers, who determine what people read in a newspaper, hear on a radio, and watch on television. For newspapers these are city desk editors, foreign editors, photo editors, community desk editors, beat reporters, and religion writers; news directors, talk show producers, and program directors in radio and assignment editors, show producers, and beat reporters in television determine what goes on the air. In each major city the Associated Press (AP.) has a local office. Local media get most of their local, regional and national news from A . P. They follow the "Daybook" prepared by AP. daybook editor. A copy of the press release should always be sent to the AP. daybook editor.

There are three main parts in almost all press releases: A lead paragraph, the main body of the release and a concluding part. News releases are now frequently sent using an e-mail address; however, it is also faxed and can also be sent via first class mail. It is always advisable to follow up by telephone and also include additional material to clarify the context. However, material should be selected judiciously and media should never be flooded with material they can not utilize. Following are some general guidelines and a check list for sending press releases.

Press Release Check list

1. Is the lead direct and to the point? Does it contain the most important and most interesting aspect of a story?
2. Has the local angle been emphasized?
3. Have who, what, when, where, why, and how been answered in the lead paragraph(s)?
4. Are sentences short, concise? Paragraphs short? Words common and concrete?
5. If there are quotations, are they natural? Do they sound as though they could have been spoken?
6. Has a particular medium format has been consistently followed?
7. Are spelling and punctuation correct?
8. Have all statements of facts being double checked for accuracy?
9. Is the release dated and is the date to be released clearly indicated?
10. Are the names and phone numbers for further contact indicated?

For newspapers a press release should follow the following format.

1. Double space and type on 8 1/2" x 11" paper.

2. Set left and right hand margin at 1 1/2" for easy editing by editors.

3. Use an official letterhead, or write the organization's name, address, and telephone number at the upper left hand corner. If the release is more than one page, center the word "more" at the bottom of the page and describe the release in a word or two at the upper left hand corner and indicate the page number. Example: Ramadan begins...2 . This is called a slug line.

4. Type the date of the release and the date to be released at the left hand side above the headlines and below the date. If it is to be immediately released, write "for immediate release."

5. List contact name and telephone number on the upper right hand corner.

6. Good releases are usually one page, or at the most two pages. Feature releases may be an exception.

7. Use only one side of a page.

8. Indent paragraphs five spaces.

9. Indicate the end of the release with either the number "30" or the symbol "###" in the center at the bottom of the final page.

10. Use a headline to localize the release (if possible) and clearly state the news hook (the needs concerns, and interest raised or satisfied).

The following Press Release was actually printed by the local newspaper in Macomb, Illinois.

Islamic Center of Macomb

334 W. Wheeler Street, Macomb, Illinois 61455.
(309) 833-3875

Press Release

March 14, 1994

Contact: Mamary Troro
295-8075

For Immediate Release

Muslims Celebrate End of Ramadan

Macomb Muslims gathered Sunday morning at the Islamic Center to celebrate the end of Ramadan -- the month of fasting. Known as Eid-ul-Fitr, this is the most joyous occasion for Muslims in the entire year. The celebration started with a prayer of thanks to almighty God and a keynote address by Dr. Mohammad Siddiqi, director of the Center.

In his speech Siddiqi emphasized the significance of the spiritual and physical experiences Muslims had during the last thirty days when they abstained from eating or taking any drink from dawn to dusk. "The purpose of this was to make us more disciplined and self restrained," said Siddiqi.

The month of fasting was a month of training and commitment to God, and this day was a day of reward from God. That is why Muslims offer their thanks to God and celebrate.

In his speech, Siddiqi also mentioned the suffering of Muslims in Bosnia, Palestine, Algeria, Kashmir and elsewhere, and he asked Muslims to pray and help these Muslims morally and materially.

Siddiqi also said that Muslims bear more responsibility to help resolve conflicts and confrontations among people of various faiths.

"The world community is under great pressure and strain. Muslims must cooperate with those who are striving to bring peace and prosperity to all human beings," Siddiqi said. "The erosion of moral values is one of the greatest threats to the survival of the human race."

Greetings were exchanged and refreshments were served to more than 60 men, women and children who attended the festivities. Gifts were presented to the children.

###

Appendix B

Media Advisory, Pitch Letter, and Letter to the Editor

Media Advisory

A media advisory or media alert provides a brief summary of the basic facts of an event and is often used to follow up the printed invitation to a special event, a news conference or a photo opportunity or often to replace it when there is no time or budget. A media advisory is always one page in length and in bold-faced type to stand out quickly to the reader. It basically answers what, where, when, and who questions. See page 114 for a sample media advisory.

Pitch Letters

If one intends to send a feature story to the media, it is always good to begin with a pitch letter the main purpose of which is to introduce the story idea and to determine if the story would be publishable in the intended media. In addition to suggesting a good story idea a pitch letter also offers substantive background information, helps set up interviews, and invites a reporter for an in-depth story about one's organization. The letter should reflect a high level of professionalism and competence. Grammar and punctuation should be perfect. If the letter is sloppy, an editor might infer that your story might also be sloppy.

One should make the pitch letter neither too formal and stuffy nor too informal and personal. The opening paragraph of a pitch letter should be good, enticing, and persuasive enough to make the editor want to read on. If an editor consistently receives good ideas and timely, useful information from some one, he or she will begin to treat such a source as reliable and trustworthy.

ABC Islamic Association

322 Main Street, Main Town, IL 61234
Telephone: 909-012-1234

June 10, 1998

Media Advisory from ABC Islamic Association

Attention: City desk editor

Contact: Abdullah Al-Abdullah
909-120-0213

Main Town Mayor Inaugurates ABC Convention

What: As the twenty first annual convention of the ABC Islamic Association begins Friday, Mayor John Jones declares this week as Muslim heritage week in Main Town, Illinois. The mayor will inaugurate the convention, which is expected to attract more than five thousand Muslims from all across the United States and Canada.

When: Friday, June 12
6:30 p.m.

Where: Main Auditorium
John Dow Convention Center
34th Street and Spruce Ave.

Who: ABC Islamic Association is a nationwide grass root organization of American Muslims with its headquarters in Anytown, USA. Its membership of over 100,000 both the indigenous and immigrant Muslims.

###

Letter to the Editor

A letter to an editor is another important way to respond to the media, especially in newspapers and magazines. These days e-mail and web-sites have made it more convenient to send immediate response in the form of letter to the editor. The following guidelines should be followed:

1. If there is no printed letterhead, one should write his/her name, address and telephone number at the top.
2. If writing on behalf of an organization, always use official stationary and provide name and phone number of the contact person.
3. Preferably, a letter to an editor should not exceed more than one page consisting of three or four paragraphs.
4. One should always write in good taste, appreciate the positives, criticize with calm, provide accurate references, and document responses whenever possible.
5. One should clearly explain if a misrepresentation was hurtful to individuals or to the community.
6. The letter should be addressed to an individual by name. One should call the particular print or broadcast media to find out who deals with letters, if the information is not already known.
7. A follow-up by phone is useful; however, if the issue is of greater importance/consequence, one should try to set up an interview in which a delegation should go if it is related to an organization.

A sample letter to the editor, addressed to the editor of *Macomb Journal* , the local newspaper in Macomb, Illinois, appears on the next page. The letter was sent on official stationary of the Islamic Center of Macomb. Follow up telephone calls were also made. The editor informed the writers of his decision to publish it. The letter was published verbatim.

Letter to the Editor

Dear Editor:

As representatives of Macomb's Muslim community, we would like to respond to the Feb. 13 article by Melisssa Sallee. We are shocked and surprised by the information, especially when it is from a respected personality as Father Keith Roderick.

Islam is based on every individual's freedom to choose between the straight path to God and the wrong one; between good and evil. The most authentic references to Islamic teachings are the Qur'an and the tradition of Prophet Muhammad. Islam is not imposed on anyone.

It is surprising to note that Father Keith is concerned about human rights violations in Pakistan, Sudan, and Iran, but has no worry about the situation in Bosnia, Kashmir, and many other parts of the world where Muslims are suffering beyond imagination.

We would like to work with Father Keith and his organization to safeguard human rights where ever they are violated. We welcome Father Keith and anyone willing to know about Islam to the Islamic Center of Macomb.

sincerely

Mamary Toro
Ismail M. Latif
Eddy Triatmodjo
Members, Muslim Students Association
Western Illinois University

Appendix C

Media Kit

A media kit is a combination of material that is prepared in advance for media practitioners who may need it as a backgrounder or as fact sheets for covering an organization's activity or for reporting an organization in special circumstances. When readily available, media kits serve as a public relations tool, as a vehicle to reach out, or simply as response material, depending on the need and nature of the occasion. A media kit usually consists of the following material:

1. A historical fact sheet giving background information of the community, group, or association.
2. A nicely written article on Islam and Muslims in America, or a set of articles dealing with various relevant issues. Chapters four and five of the book may very well be used for this purpose.
3. A list of office bearers including their brief biographical backgrounds.
4. A calendar of important events outlining the nature of each event.
5. Any brochure, folders, pamphlets, and current copy of newsletter, if available.
6. Photographs of office bearers, centers, mosques, and important events of the past.
7. A press release in case of a special event that media are invited to cover. A video news release (VNR) if the kit is sent to a television station.
8. A good video program of an activity in the past if available.
9. A covering letter addressed, in person, to the news/feature, community or religion editor.
10. A rolodex card, if possible, with name and phone numbers of media resource persons.

Appendix D

News Conference and Special Events

A news conference is often used as the opportunity for conveying the target audience important news through media, and also to cultivate good media relations. Depending on the impact and the news worthiness of the subject, a news conference may be the best way to give out a story simultaneously to all media. The news conference should be called only after making the determination that there is enough breaking news that most of the invited media reporters will attend. Even though a news conference is the most straight forward method for generating news and publicity, the result may be disappointing if there is not enough news that can attract media coverage. It is important to plan a news conference effectively and in great detail, as one would plan for a special event. The following checklist may be useful in successful organization of a news conference or a special or big media event.

1. Establish the desired outcome or the goals to be accomplished.
2. Determine themes, approaches and tie-ins.
3. Make an appropriate list of media and other invitees.
4. Make a detailed and time-bound schedule for pre-publicity -- press release, media kit, backgrounders, media advisory, and photo-opportunity alert.
5. Carefully plan for logistical details of arrangements -- light, sound, seating, distribution materials and timing for distribution, and refreshments and food if any.
6. Send invitations at least two weeks ahead. Follow them up by telephone after a week and again at least a day before the event.
7. Train the person or persons who will be at center stage. Make at least two rehearsals of the entire event. Prepare possible questions from media and draft answers.
8. Make a plan for interviews. Reporters appreciate the courtesy of making individual officials available for interview during a defined period of time.

9. It is good to have visuals to explain a point of view. This may include charts, graphics, pictures, slides, and overheads.

10. Make a crisis plan too. This means if for any reason the event does not go as planned, what will be done to gain maximum results. In addition to plan A, there should at least be a plan B and a plan C.

Appendix E

Examples of Good Media Coverage

Chicago Tribune
Founded June 10, 1847
Scott C. Smith, *Publisher* Howard A. Tyner, *Editor*
N. Don Wycliff, *Editorial Page Editor* Ann Marie Lipinski, *Managing Editor*
James O'Shea, *Deputy Managing Editor/News* Gerould Kern, *Deputy Managing Editor/Features*
R. Bruce Dold, *Deputy Editorial Page Editor* F. Richard Ciccone, *Associate Editor*
Section 1 Friday, June 19, 1998

A new brand of American justice?

Mohammad Salah may be every bit the terrorist the United States government suggests he is. But so far, nobody has proved it by clear and convincing evidence in an open court of law. On the contrary, the government seems to have adopted an approach toward Salah of punishment first, trial later.

That's wrong. It's unfair. It is, if we may use the term, un-American. The government owes Salah an immediate, fair and open trial at which the evidence against him can be presented and rebutted. And it needs in the meantime to return the property that it has seized from him.

Not just Mohammad Salah's rights are at stake in this case, but those of every American.

Salah, a naturalized American citizen from suburban Bridgeview, had his home and the assets of an Islamic literacy organization with which he is associated—some $1.3 million in property all told—seized last week by FBI agents.

The reason: They allegedly were proceeds of a scheme in which money was funneled into the U.S. from abroad, to be laundered in American banks and then transferred to Hamas, the militant Palestinian organization that has waged a campaign of terror against Israel.

The government accomplished the seizure under the laws on civil forfeiture, which technically make the property, not the owner, the defendant in such actions. This is, of course, a fiction in every sense except the legal one. Civil forfeiture has given us heartburn in other contexts. It is used most commonly in drug cases. Salah's is, according to U.S. Atty. Scott Lassar, the first application of the laws in an anti-terrorism case.

What Mohammad Salah now must do is go to court and prove that he is *not* a terrorist, *not* a money-launderer and that the government ought *not* have his property. This Mohammad-through-the-looking-glass scenario is not the American way of justice most of us learned in grade school civics. Silly us, huh? We actually believed in that due-process, innocent-until-proven-guilty business.

The case against Salah—or, if you prefer, against his assets—rests in no small part on his conviction in an Israeli military court several years ago for channeling funds to Hamas. That conviction, for which he served five years in prison, was based on a confession obtained under questioning behind closed doors and without benefit of even the pretense of due process.

It's possible to understand how Israel, a nation under siege, might persuade itself that that is justice. It's impossible to understand how America could.

Los Angeles Times
SUNDAY, JANUARY 22, 1995

Islamic Leaders Urge Respect for Diversity

■ **Religion:** Worries arise that anti-Muslim feelings will increase after Jewish groups ask government to crack down on terrorism.

By LARRY B. STAMMER
TIMES RELIGION WRITER

Worried that calls by two Jewish organizations for a government crackdown on terrorists could lead to widespread civil rights violations against all Muslims, the leaders of six Islamic groups issued a joint declaration Saturday urging respect for American pluralism.

The declaration comes amid growing concern among Muslim Americans and Islamic leaders over what they see as a renewal of negative stereotyping of Muslims in the United States.

Anti-Muslim feeling last hit a peak and then subsided after the 1993 bombing of the World Trade Center in New York. Four Muslims were found guilty last March of conspiracy in that incident.

Meeting at the Islamic Center of Southern California in Los Angeles, Muslim leaders Saturday took a strong stand against terrorism, as they have before, and deplored "indecency committed against any human being." They also issued a plea for continued dialogue with Christians, Jews and other non-Muslims.

Still, they have been outraged, they said, by the tone of a new call by the American Jewish Committee in New York urging the new Congress and the Clinton Administration to "combat the activities of radical Islamic terrorism."

Among other things, the Jewish group asked the government last month to block individuals and groups in the United States from sending financial contributions to Hamas, Hezbollah and "other militant Islamic extremist groups."

At the same time, the Simon Wiesenthal Center in Los Angeles urged President Clinton to order the Justice Department to investigate "groups posing as legitimate organizations that are actually fronts for Hamas."

The calls by the two Jewish groups came after members of Hamas kidnaped and murdered an Israeli soldier, Nachshon Waxman, and bombed a bus in Tel Aviv, killing 22 Israelis in October.

Islamic leaders said the American Jewish Committee's language was so sweeping that the vast majority of innocent, law-abiding Muslim Americans could be unfairly targeted by government investigators and the public. Ultimately, they said, respect for American pluralism was at stake.

"We are Americans to the core and we want a piece of the pie," Maher Hathout of the Islamic Center of Southern California said [illegible]

[illegible]

The New York Times

SUNDAY, MAY 2, 1993

A Growing Presence, Muslims Proclaim Their Differences

Some of Islam's many races and nationalities after praying together in Manhattan at the end of Ramadan.

Many Muslims say they are struggling with the sometimes-conflicting the demands of assimilating into the American mainstream while at the same time sustaining a separate Muslim identity. Their quest is complicated by some special problems: there is a widespread view of Islam as an old fashioned religion, prone to violence, intolerant of non-Muslims and demeaning to women. While many Muslims deny that these features actually exist in Islam, there are tensions between some traditional Muslim beliefs and many customs of American life.

A Growing Islamic Presence: Balancing Sacred and Secular

By RICHARD BERNSTEIN
Special to The New York Times

LOS ANGELES — About 100 miles north of here in the cornucopia of the San Joaquin Valley, Ali Hamdhe, who was born in Yemen, runs a Frosty King where the familiar meets the new. Kids in sneakers and baseball hats mingle with men in skull caps and desert robes, eating hamburgers and tacos. At the end of the day, the men go to a mosque in a converted warehouse where they read frayed copies of the Koran and say the evening prayers.

Here in Los Angeles, Abdul Karim Hasan, who was born in New Jersey and converted to Islam after hearing Malcolm X preach, is the imam of the Masjid Felix Bilal. This mosque, with a growing congregation in the heart of the city's biggest black neighborhood, is building a larger edifice with money provided by Saudi Arabia.

Numbers May Surpass Jews

Imam Hasan was preparing for a trip to Mecca and to Egypt, where he was to receive an award for his contribution to Islam in America.

These are two of the varied faces of a growing Islamic presence in America [illegible]

Muslims in America

First of two articles.

waves of immigration and the conversion of large numbers of black Americans has led to a surge in the number of Muslims. There are now more than 1,100 mosques in the United States; almost every state has at least one, and a recent study indicated that about 80 percent had been founded within the last 12 years.

About a billion people, or a fifth of the earth's population, are Muslims, but in this country, the number is elusive. The best estimates put the population of Muslims in America at three million to four million. If recent trends continue, they are likely to surpass the six million Jews here sometime early in the next century.

In the American tradition, Muslims here both proclaim their differences and strive to fit in; they have become a significant new part of the national mosaic.

"Islam is an American religion," said Prof. Yvonne Y. Haddad, an expert in Islamic studies at the University of Massachusetts, who sees Islam taking on an American flavor, and at the same time influencing the nation's culture. Many thousands of American citizens face Mecca and pray to Allah five times a day, and some girls in public schools are wearing head covers in traditional Muslim fashion. There are tens of thousands of children for whom religious education is not catechism or lessons in Hebrew, but an introduction to the Five Pillars of Islam and the Arabic language.

When it comes to domestic politics, "We are both Democrats and Republicans," said Maher Mohammed Hathout, an Egyptian-born cardiologist and the chairman of the Islamic Center of Southern California. "We are politically liberal but socially conservative. We believe in the duty of the state to help people, but we are anti-abortion, anti-pornography, against sex outside of marriage, in favor of family values."

As'ad AbuKhalil, a scholar in residence at the Middle East Institute in Washington, stresses the diversity among Muslims but allows that as Islamic influence grows and becomes organized, it is likely to be on the conservative side.

Coalition of Conservatives?

"There are those of us who pray and others who get drunk at night and stuff dollar bills into the costumes of belly dancers," he said. "I wouldn't be surprised years from now to see a fundamentalist front comprising Muslims, Christians and Jews united over things like drugs, pornography, abortion and other issues."

The Population

Keeping Identity But Adapting, Too

Like other immigrant and religious groups, Muslims tend to feel more deeply than other Americans about certain issues. Many identify with the struggles of Muslims overseas, like the Palestinians, Bosnians and Kashmiris.

Especially after the bombing of the World Trade Center in New York City, people from public commentators to private citizens have asked whether Muslim extremists who hate the United States and are obsessed with Middle Eastern politics may be insinuating themselves deeply into the nation's Muslim population, making the United States more vulnerable to terrorism.

But most Muslims in the United States say they are like any other group, seeking freedom and prosperity. The immigrants are eager to adapt but at the same time retain a separate religious identity.

"We feel proud of our American Islamic identity," Dr. Hathout said. "We want to be part of the mosaic. We don't consider ourselves to belong to the Middle East or to South Asia. Our roots are there but our present and our future are here."

Two-Thirds Are Immigrants

While estimates of the number of American Muslims range widely and no one is sure, Dr. Haddad of the University of Massachusetts thinks the estimate of three million to four million is the most reliable. Of these, she said, perhaps two-thirds are immigrants or their offspring and one-third American-born converts.

Like total numbers, accurate statistics on the growth in Islam are hard to come by. New arrivals to the United States are not classified by religion, and it is not accurate to simply count the people who come from countries with large Muslim populations, because many of them are not Muslims.

Still, taking 1991 as an example, there were more than 100,000 legal immigrants from countries with substantial Muslim populations, like Pakistan, India, Egypt, Bangladesh, Iran and Lebanon, and a substantial percentage of those were certainly Muslims. Moreover, there are unknown numbers of illegal immigrants who are Muslims.

At the Islamic Resource Institute in Orange County, California, Ihsan Bagby, a black convert to Islam who was born in Cleveland, has been conducting a survey of all mosques in America. His early findings indicate that there are more than 1,100 of them and that about 80 percent were founded in the last 12 years. Dr. Bagby estimates that 30 percent of Muslims in the country are black.

6 The Macomb Journal, Friday, March 18, 1994

Inspirations

Photo Special to the Journal

Muslims embrace each other after prayers at the Islamic Center in Macomb.

Muslims mark end of Ramadan

Special to the Journal

Macomb — Macomb Muslims gathered Sunday morning at the Islamic Center to celebrate the end of Ramadan — the month of fasting.

Known as the Eid, this is the most joyous occasion for Muslims in the entire year. The celebrations started with a prayer of thanks to almighty God and a keynote address by Dr. Mohammad Siddiqi, director of the center.

In his address, Siddiqi emphasized the significance of the spiritual and physical experiences that Muslims had during the last thirty days, which is when they abstained from eating or taking any drink from dawn to dusk.

"The pupose of this was to make us more disciplined and self-restrained," Siddiqi said.

The month of fasting was a month of training and commitment to God, and this day was the day of reward from God. That is why Muslims offer their thanks to God and celebrate.

In his speech, Siddiqi also mentioned the suffering of Muslims in Bosnia, Palestine, Algeria, Kashmir and elsewhere, and he asked Muslims to pray and help them morally and materially.

Siddiqi also said that Muslims bear more responsibility to help resolve conflicts and confrontations among people of various faiths.

"The world community is under great pressure and strain, and Muslims must cooperate with those who are striving to bring peace and prosperity for all human beings," Siddiqi said. "The erosion of moral values is one of the greatest threats to the survival of the human race."

Greetings were exchanged and refreshments were served to more than 60 men, women and children who attended the festivities. Gifts were presented to the children.

Friday
March 18, 1994
MACOMB JOURN
Local Newspaper Serving Macomb, Illinois, Since 1856 Copyright 1994 © A Park Newspaper 128 N. Lafayette St., 61455

USA TODAY · WEDNESDAY [illegible]

OPINION USA

The World Trade Center bombing has prompted hearings in Congress over fears about terrorism and has raised concerns in the Muslim community that old stereotypes are resurfacing. USA TODAY asked expert Yvonne Haddad for her perspective

Islam is about peace, not violence

Muslims are unfairly tagged as terrorists, and the press is part of the problem. 'Islamic terrorism sells,' says professor.

WHAT IS ISLAM?

Yvonne Haddad is professor of Islamic history at the University of Massachusetts, Amherst. Her comments on Islam were edited from an interview with USA TODAY's Sharon Shahid.

The word Islam comes from the three-letter root word in Arabic, "slm," which stands for peace. And, in a sense, Islam is the religion of peace. That's just the way the Koran talks about it — the religion of peace. When you become a Muslim, you become at peace with God, and that's what Islam means, to surrender to God, to stop fighting God. To be at peace with him, to have a relationship of peace. People should know that Islam, in a sense, urges people to worship the same God that Christianity and Judaism do. That we share not only the same God, but the same perception about accountability in this life. The accountability at the end of time on Earth. And also for the way we live our lives. It also calls for brotherhood and understanding, and it's very hard to teach that because most people have a prejudiced idea about what it is at the moment.

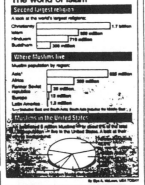

HADDAD

FEAR OF TERRORISM

When we first came to this country, the stereotype of Islam or Muslims in America was camel jockeys, insignificant, on the margin of civilization. In the '70s after the oil boycott, the stereotype became one of what I call the oil sheik, someone who's a threat to our way of life because he wants to increase the price of oil. And then in the '80s, it became the terrorist. When I went into class this semester and I asked my students, "What comes to your head when I ask what is a Muslim, they said terrorists."

If we look back, we can see that it goes back to 1979 with the coming of the Ayatollah Khomeini with the vision of Muslims in Iran saying, "Death to America," that kind of stuff. It's ascribed to Muslims. I'm not saying that there aren't some terrorists who happen to be Muslims. All I'm saying is you can't tag the whole religion with it. The definition of a Muslim is one who prays. And so, terrorism is equated to any Muslim who takes his religion seriously. It is a very important thing to teach people in this country that we cannot demonize a religion, to have people afraid to pray.

COMPARING WITH WACO

If you look at the United States, there are people killing people all day long. We don't say that there are Christians out killing people, do we? Look at Waco, Texas. Does that stand for Christianity? No. We don't talk about Christianity as a religion of violence because there's a crazy man in Waco. We don't talk about Christianity as a terrorist religion because there's the Ku Klux Klan, which goes around carrying a cross and saying, "We are doing this in the name of Christ." We distinguish between the acts of terrorist Christians and Christianity. There is a tendency in the American press — and there are a variety of reasons for it — to associate Islam with terrorism. It's unfair. I'm not a Muslim myself, I'm a Christian, and I feel it's sort of unfair. If a Muslim man beats his wife, then they say "Muslims beat their wives." When a Christian beats his wife, they say, "This man beats his wife." They don't say, "Christianity teaches the beating of wives." The impression is that all women are beaten up. They're all oppressed. You look at American society and you see how many women get beaten. Nobody says that Christianity encourages the beating of women.

The world of Islam

Second largest religion

A look at the world's largest religions:

Christianity	1.7 billion
Islam	[illegible] million
Hinduism	719 million
Buddhism	[illegible] million

Where Muslims live

Muslim population by region:

Asia[1]	[illegible] million
Africa	[illegible] million
Former Soviet republics	30 million
Europe	13 million
Latin America	1.3 million

1 — Includes East and South Asia; South Asia includes the Middle East

Muslims in the United States

An estimated 6 million Muslims — or about [illegible]% of the total U.S. population — live in the United States. A look at their ethnic background:

[illegible]

By Elys A. McLean, USA TODAY

ROLE OF THE PRESS

The press needs to sell stories, and Islamic terrorism sells. There are some newspapers that do it more carefully than others, but it keeps being used. And it has repercussions in the Muslim community in the United States.

We don't know what the [World Trade Center] bombing in New York is. We have absolutely no idea whether this guy (suspect Mohammed Salameh) did it or not. But already there seems to be a presumption of guilt and association with the mosque in New Jersey. We don't know that this guy ever went to that mosque or whether he heard him (cleric Omar Abdel Rahman) preach. The press has tried the guy and found him guilty already. And as far as I can tell, there is very circumstantial evidence.

The press needs to do a more fair description of what is happening. The press has gone a little haywire on this one. It's been overdramatized. The press is drawing maps about terrorism, and the implication is that "they're here in the United States and they're about to take over." For Muslims living in this country, it's kind of scary.

MUSLIMS IN USA

There are Muslims who are in their 5th generation of immigrants in the United States. The records I've been lecturing with show unequivocally that Muslims have fought in the First World War, Second World War, Korean War, Vietnam War and in Operation Desert Storm.

It's also true for immigrants who have left their countries recently that they have some identification with the country they left. This is no different from any other immigrant group. It doesn't mean that these Muslims — who live in this country because of economic, political or religious reasons — are terrorists or are anti-American. What I'm saying is not because I'm a Muslim, I'm saying that because it is my research interest. I'm an Arab-Christian. Everybody thinks I'm a Muslim because my name is Haddad. There are over 2 million Arab-Christians in the United States. They get bashed with the Muslims just because of their last names.

MYTHS

Haddad was asked to clear up some other misconceptions. Here is what she had to say about:

Women aren't equal in the religion of Islam. According to the teachings of the Koran, God created man and woman of the same cell. They're supposed to be equal. They are equal in the sight of God. The distinction is in their [illegible]. Every unit must have a leader, and the man is seen as the leader. When you have to make a final decision in the Islamic system, the husband [illegible] the last decision.

Women can't drive. The other day I had an interview and the reporter was asking me questions. And he said, "Well, Muslim women cannot drive." That is nonsense. There are about [illegible] Muslims in the world. There are about 50 Muslim countries. There is one country — Saudi Arabia — that doesn't allow women to drive. And suddenly [illegible] women cannot [illegible]. Muslim women drive all over the world except Saudi Arabia.

Muslims come from the Mideast. The Arabs are 15% of the Muslim population of the world. There are only about 150,000 Muslims in the world [illegible] majority of Muslims is [illegible] Arab. In fact, there are more Indonesian Muslims than Arab Muslims.

The holy war. The holy war is a very interesting [illegible] because the word [illegible] has come to mean holy war in American terminology. But in Islam, there is an interpretation of the lesser jihad and the higher jihad. The lesser jihad is war, and the higher jihad is more important. It is the struggle of the self, the relationship with God and still the tendency to evil. That is the great struggle of the human being. The lesser jihad is war, is sanctioned in conditions when Muslims are subjected to [illegible].

Fundamentalism. Fundamentalism is an [illegible] word to use [illegible] there is no Arabic [illegible] fundamentalism [illegible] mentalism is a [illegible] word. Fundamentalism [illegible] come to mean [illegible] some [illegible] public

New York Times

NEW YORK, MONDAY, AUGUST 28, 1995

Amid Islam's Growth in the U.S., Muslims Face a Surge in Attacks

Survey of Mosques Documents the Hate Crimes

By JAMES BROOKE

SPRINGFIELD, Ill., Aug. 25 — The city's mosque had burned, gasoline-fueled flames melting the vinyl siding, charring the prayer hall, and scorching the rooftop crescent. But Aamir Markinson decided to pray in the empty parking lot, behind the yellow police tape.

"I finished praying, looked up, and saw three teen-age girls standing at the gate," recalled the 30-year-old mother, who stands out in this small Midwestern city because she wears a hijab, the head scarf of a devout Muslim.

First came the jeers: "They should just give it up" and "Why don't you just go home?"

Then, as Mrs. Markinson's pace quickened down the sidewalk that June afternoon, the stones came.

"I had felt that antipathy in Germany, when they would say, 'Go home, you dirty Turk,'" said Mrs. Markinson, a former member of the Army military police who converted to Islam after serving in the Gulf war. "But this is Springfield."

Springfield, where Abraham Lincoln alerted pre-Civil War America with a speech on "A House Divided," is again witness to a pernicious division spreading across the land: a surge in hate crimes against Muslims.

During the past year, five American mosques have been burned down or seriously vandalized. In the three days after the Oklahoma City bombing in April, an anti-defamation group recorded 222 attacks against Muslims — ranging from spitting on women wearing shawls to death threats to shots fired at mosques to a fake bomb thrown at a Muslim day care center.

On April 19, the day of the bombing, many American television stations indicated that Islamic fundamentalists were the prime suspects. The two men indicted for the crime, Timothy J. McVeigh and Terry L. Nichols, are American-born and are considered to have been driven by right-wing politics, not religious fervor.

The increasing vandalism and attacks are considered to be only a glimpse of the broader picture. "Only 10 percent of the mosques responded to our survey," said Ibrahim Hooper, spokesman for the Council on American-Islamic Relations. The council, based in Washington, released its report on Thursday. The group's next project is to prepare a booklet on mosque security and distribute it to the roughly 1,500 mosques in the United States.

The increase in hate crimes comes

Continued on Page B7, Column 1

0 JUNE 8, 1998 • CRAIN'S CHICAGO BUSINESS

Growing Muslim community makes its mark

1USLIMS *from Page 1*

lation continues to grow—creat-
ıg an expanding spiritual and eco-
omic infrastructure to support a
ıetro-area Muslim population
ıat has increased by about one-
ıird in the past decade alone.

The exact number of Muslims
ere is hard to determine. The
arliament of the World's Reli-
ons estimates the number of
luslims in Illinois at 350,000 to
·00,000. Muslim political groups
·timate higher, while Muslim re-
gious representatives tend to es-
mate lower. In the Chicago
ıetropolitan area, the consensus
ıess is just over 400,000 Mus-
ıns, up from about 300,000 a
·cade ago.

"It's the fastest-growing reli-
ous community in the Chicago
ea," says Dirk Ficca, the parlia-
ent's executive director.

About half of the newcomers are clustered around the mosque on the city's South Side, and shops can be found in Schaumburg, Elgin and Orland Park.

"Every year, someone opens a new shop," says Arshad Khan, who runs Noor Meat Market on Devon Avenue.

But in spite of the increased competition, Mr. Khan says sales are up. In 1996, he and brother Amjad moved their store to a new, 3,000-square-foot location—three times the size of its former site.

Larger food distributors like Chicago's Olympia Food Industries Inc., which makes meat for gyros, and Deerfield-based My Own Meals Inc., which makes a halal-certified beef stew and a variety of other products, are also targeting the Muslim market.

It's still a small niche, says My Own Meals President Mary Anne Jackson, who originally developed the halal meal for the U.S. military, but it is growing enough for the company to make long-range plans. "The market is in its infancy, but it's starting," Ms. Jackson says.

The Muslim presence is especially large in the food industry.

The company currently exports most of its halal products, but is planning to sell products in the U.S. starting next month.

Olympia started supplying halal products to restaurants three years ago and has seen annual sales grow 20% a year. The company plans to package an all-halal gyro kit—meat, pita and sauce—and have it on grocery store shelves by yearend, says President Andre Papantoniou. "It's a growing market with a lot of potential."

Elk Grove Village-based UAL Corp., parent of United Airlines, began offering halal meals in 1991. Muslim fliers who once had to settle for the fruit plate now can get couscous with raisins and tomato concasse.

Part of food service expansion can be explained by the boom in processed and prepared foods, says Muhammad Munir Chaudry, a former food chemist who now heads the Chicago-based Islamic Food and Nutrition Council of America.

Twenty years ago, shoppers try-

A12 Austin American-Statesman — Sunday, February 21, [illegible]

Growing Muslim population looks to heritage for guidance

Continued from A1

has adopted a similar philosophy.

"Islam is not a personal opinion. It's not something I have to analyze, to think of. It's decision. Everything was sent by God and the Prophet Mohammed," he said. "We are not children of God, but servants of God. He does not need us, we need him."

Islam is reported to be the fastest-growing religion in the world. The number of Muslims in Austin has grown to an estimated [illegible], statistics show. The majority moved to the United States from the Middle East and Pakistan.

Although the Muslim faith is frequently associated with the Middle East, that region is home only to about 18 percent of the 1.2 billion followers of Islam worldwide. The largest Muslim communities are in Indonesia, followed by the Indian subcontinent, including India, Pakistan and Bangladesh. In addition, there are substantial and growing Muslim populations in Malaysia and in such African nations as Somalia and Sudan.

National statistics also show the number of Muslims living in Western nations is on the rise. Their presence is evident on every continent and in every large Western city — from Austin and Atlanta to Leeds, England, and Lyon, France. The United States is home to an estimated 7 million to 8 million Muslims. But the degree to which they follow the dictates of their religion varies widely. Equally disparate are the customs they follow. And in many cases, their traditions are not necessarily rooted in Islam but in their native lands.

Over the past few years, for example, women in Saudi Arabia have complained they are being treated as second-class citizens. Authorities in Canada are debating granting asylum to a Saudi Arabian woman who says she will be persecuted if she returns home. It is Saudi Arabian laws that are in dispute, not the requirements of Islam.

There are two main sects of Islam. The dominant Sunni branch and the Shiites, who live mainly in Iran and surrounding countries. Although there is a perception that some sects are more militant than others, the fundamentalism that sometimes is associated with Islam does not stem from the religion but from political movements within various countries where Muslims dominate the population.

Muslim families in Austin deal with their experiences, their heritage and their beliefs in individual ways. But they share a common thread. They all believe they must submit to the will of God, or Allah as he is known in Arabic. It is their perception and interpretation of that will that varies.

Like many other Muslims who have immigrated to the United States, primarily in search of education and employment, El Nasr and her husband, Mahmoud, a 38-year-old engineer employed by IBM, have held firm to the culture and religion of their homeland. And they are striving to embed those values in their children, two boys and two girls, aged 2 to 7.

"Some families have had a hard time," said Basmah El Nasr, who is sympathetic to the struggle Muslims have faced trying to adapt to the United States while clinging to their roots.

Hossam Aylouch, a senior at the University of Texas and the president of the Muslim Student Association, shares Basmah El Nasr's philosophies. Aylouch,

---

[illegible]er 20, 1987 Chicago Tribune
Religion

Moslems keep open mind on open diets

By Anwar Iqbal

If it's true that you are what you eat, then Moslems in the United States have a problem. Shops are full of food, but all that is sold in the supermarkets and restaurants is not for Moslems.

Islam's dietary laws restrict their choice. Alcoholic drinks are banned. So is pork. Even biscuits and pillies using animal fat are on the banned list. So are all kinds of meat—beef, poultry or mutton—if the animal is not slaughtered in Islamic fashion.

So what to eat?

Ulema, or scholars, of five major Moslem sects—Hanafi, Maliki, Hanbli, Shafai and Shiite—met in Chicago's Moslem Community Center earlier this week to consider Islamic dietary laws. And they concluded that all meat sold in a supermarket is *halal*, or permissible for a Moslem to eat, except pork.

This pronouncement is likely to be welcomed by many of America's 8 million Moslems, who find it difficult to observe dietary laws in secular society. On the other hand, traditional Moslems might be angered.

The organizers of the symposium realized the possibility of causing a bitter controversy. Rashid Choudhary, president of the Islamic Food and Nutrition Council of America, which organized the meeting, announced after the discussion that he and his council remain faithful to the traditional dietary concepts.

Some in the audience also disagreed, like Mohammad Hussain Zaidi, the Shiite scholar, who said: "I am not willing to eat *haram* [prohibited food] simply because it is available in the supermarket."

Even those who did not disagree with the conclusion were surprised. They did not expect traditional scholars to make such a pronouncement.

Shaik Mohammed Nur Abdullah leads the discussion at an Islamic symposium on dietary laws and contemporary issues

But nobody was as surprised and pleased as the *halal* meat merchants. "We have to buy *halal* meat from special butchers at a very high rate and have to sell it at little profit to compete with the supermarkets," said Mohammad Qureshi, one merchant. "Now we can buy cheap meat and sell it competitive rates."

Though a pronouncement like this in an Islamic country might cause public wrath against the scholars, there were many at Sunday's symposium who understood the need for it.

Dr. Mohammad Adam, a former sharia (Islamic laws) judge from the Sudan and now director and prayer leader at Baltimore's Islamic Center, was one of them.

"The modern way of life is compelling us to do a lot of things which were not done before, such as machine slaughter," he said. "The need for re-interpretation of Islamic laws is stronger now than it has ever been. The dilemma is how to adopt modern means without disturbing the fundamental values of Islam."

The issue of *halal* or *haram* (permissible and non-permissible food), he says, should not be separated from other issues.

"A lot of things have changed since the advent of Islam 1,400 years ago," he said. "It will be unfair to religion to insist that since the Prophet Mohammad and his companions traveled on camels, we should do the same."

Though there are other things that are considered not fit for eating by Moslems, the issue of *halal* meat is a big concern for those living in the United States or Europe.

Islam allows a Moslem to eat the meat of most farm animals provided they are slaughtered in the traditional way.

Moslems believe that it is obligatory for them to say the name of Allah while slaughtering an animal, to use a very sharp knife and to cut the neck in a particular way to spare the animal pain.

Because the meat sold in supermarkets is not slaughtered in this manner, it has been considered *haram*. Most Moslems don't buy the supermarket meat. Instead, they buy from special *halal* meat shops.

Appendix F
National Broadcast Media Directory

1. *ABC News*
77 W. 66th Street
New York, NY 10023
(212) 456-7777

2. *ABC Radio Network*
125 West End Ave.
New York, NY 10023
(212) 456-1000

3. *AP Network News*
1825 K Street N.W., # 710
Washington, DC. 20006700
(202) 736-1100

4.*CBN (Christian Broadcasting Network)*
CBN Center
Virginia Beach, VA 23463
(804) 424--7777

5. *CBS News / CBS Radio Network*
51 W. 52nd Street
New York, NY 10019
(212) 975-4321

6. *CNN News / CNN Radio Network*
1 CNN Center
Atlanta, GA 30348
(404) 827-1503

7. *Corporation for Public Broadcasting*
901 E Street NW.
Washington, DC 20004
(202) 879-9600

8. *ESPN Radio Inc.*
ESPN Plaza
935 Middle street
Bristol, CT 06001
(203) 585-2000

9. *Fox Broadcasting Co.*
10201 West Pico Blvd.
Los Angeles, CA 90035
(310) 369-3553

10. *Mutual Broadcasting Network*
1755 S. Jefferson Davis Hwy.
Arlington, VA 22202
(703) 413-8300

11. *NBC News*
30 Rockefeller Plaza
New York, NY 10112
(212) 664-4444

12. *National Public Radio (NPR)*
635 Massachusetts Ave. NW.
Washington, DC. 20001
(202) 879- 9600

13. *PBS (Public Broadcasting Service)*
1320 Baraddock Plaza
Alexandria, VA 22314
(703) 739-5000

Appendix G
National News Magazines and Major Newspapers with Full Time Religion Writers / Editors

1. *The Arizona Republic*
120 E. Van Buren Street
Phoenix, AZ 85005
(602) 271-8000

2. *The Atlanta Journal Constitution*
72 Marietta St. NW.
P. O. Box 4689
Atlanta, GA 30302
(800) 846-6672
(404) 526- 5746 (fax)

3. *Baltimore Sun*
Clavert & Centre Sts.
Baltimore, MD 21278
(410) 332-6000
(410) 752-6049 (fax)

4. *Boston Globe*
135 Morrissey Blvd.
Boston, MA 02107
(617) 929-2935
(617) 929-3192 (fax)

5. *Chicago Sun-Times*
401 N. Wabash Ave.
Chicago, IL 60611
(312) 321-3000
(312) 321-3084 (fax)

6. *Chicago Tribune*
435 N. Michigan Ave.
Chicago, IL 60611
(312) 222-3232

7. *Christian Science Monitor*
One Norway Street
Boston, MA 02115
(617) 450-2000
(617) 450-7575 (fax)

8. *The Cincinnati Enquirer*
312 Elm St.
Cincinnati, OH 45202
(513) 721-2700
(513) 721-2703 (fax)

9. *The Columbus Dispatch*
34 S. Third St.
Columbus, OH 43215
(614) 461-5000
(614) 461-7580

10. *The Dallas Morning News*
508 Young Street
Dallas, TX 75265
(214) 977-8222
(214) 977-8638 (fax)

11. *Dayton Daily News*
45 S. Ludlow St.
Dayton, OH 45401
(513) 225-2321
(513) 225-2334 (fax)

12. *The Denver Post*
1650 Broadway
Denver, CO 80202
(303) 820-1010
(303) 832-4609 (fax)

13. *Detroit Free Press*
321 W. Lafayette Blvd.
Detroit, MI 48231
(313) 222-6400
(313) 222-5981 (fax)

14. *The Detroit News*
615 W. Lafayette Blvd.
Detroit, MI 48226
(313) 222-2300
(313) 222-2335(fax)

15. *The Florida Times- Union*
P.O.Box 1949
Jacksonville, FL 32231
(904) 359-4111
(904) 359-4478 (fax)

16. *Fort Worth Star-Telegram*
P.O.Box 1870
Ft. Worth, TX 76101
(817) 390-7400
(817(390-7831(fax)

17. *The Fresno Bee*
1626 E. St.
Fresno, CA 93786
(209) 441-6436
(209) 441-6111(fax)

18. *The Grand Rapids Press*
155 Michigan St. N. W.
Grand Rapids, MI 49503
(616) 459-1400
(616) 459-1502 (fax)

19. *The Hartford Courant*
285 Broad Street
Hartford, CT 06115
(860) 241-6200
(860) 520-3176 (fax)

20. *Houston Chronicle*
801 Texas Street
Houston, TX 77002
(713)220-7171
(713)220-6677 (fax)

21. *The Houston Post*
4747 Southwest Freeway
P.O.Box 4747
Houston, TX 77210-4747
(713) 840-5600
(713) 840-6722 (fax)

22. *The Kansas City Star*
1729 Grand Ave.
Kansas City, MO 64108
(816) 234-4141
(816) 234-4926 (fax)

23. *The Miami Herald*
One Herald Plaza
Miami, Fl 33101
(305) 350-2111

24. *Los Angeles Times*
Times Mirror Square
Los Angeles, CA 90053
(213) 237-5000
(213) 237-7910 (fax)

25. *The Morning News Tribune*
1950 S. State Street
P.O.Box 11000
Tacoma, WA 98411
(206) 597-8742
(206) 597-8266 (fax)

26. *The New York Times*
229 West 43rd Street
New York, NY 10036
(212) 556-1234

27. *Pittsburgh Post Gazette*
50 Blvd. of the Allies
Pittsburgh, PA 15222
(412) 263-1100
(412) 391-8452 (fax)

28. *The Philadelphia Enquirer*
400 N. Broad Street
Philadelphia, PA 19103
(215) 854-2000
215) 854-4794 (fax)

29. *Providence Journal Bulletin*
75 Fountain street
Providence, RI 02902
(401) 277-7000
(401) 277-7889 (fax)

30. *The Plain Dealer*
1801 Superior Ave. E
Cleveland, OH 44114
(216) 344-4600
(216) 344-4620 (fax)

31. *Rocky Mountain News*
400 W. Colfax Ave.
P.O.Box 719
Denver, CO 80201
(800) 933-1990
(303) 892-5081 (fax)

32. *Richmond Times-Dispatch*
333 E. Grace Street
Richmond, VA 23219
(804) 649-6000
(804) 775-8059 (fax)

33. *St. Petersburg Times*
P.O.Box 1121
St. Petersburg, Fl. 33731
(813) 893-8111
(813) 893-8675 (fax)

34. *St. Pual Pioneer Press*
345 Cedar Street
St. Paul, MN 55101
(612) 222-5011
(612) 228-5500 (fax)

35. *The San Diego Union-Tribune*
350 Camino de la Reina
San Diego, CA 92108
(619) 299-3131
(619) 299-1440 (fax)

36. *San Antonio Express-News*
Ave. E & 3rd Street
P.O.Box 2171-7297
San Antonio, TX 78205
(210) 225-7411
(210) 225-8351 (fax)

38. *San Francisco Chronicle*
901 Mission Street
San Francisco, CA 94103
(415) 777-1111
(415) 896-1107 (fax)

39. *San Jose Mercury News*
750 Ridder Park Drive
San Jose, CA 95190
(408) 920-5000
(408) 288-8060(fax)

40. *The Seattle Times*
P.O.Box 70
Seattle, WA 98111
(206) 464-2111
(206) 464-2261 (fax)

41. *The Star-Ledger*
One Star Ledger Plaza
Newark, NJ 07102
(201) 877-4141
(201) 877-5845 (fax)

42. *The Tennessean*
1100 Broadway
Nashville, TN 37203
(615) 259-8000
(615) 259-8093 (fax)

43. *U.S.A. Today*
1100 Wilson Blvd.
Arlington, VA 22234
(703) 276-3400
(703) 558-4646 (fax)

44. *The Wall Street Journal*
420 Lexington Ave.
New York, NY 10170
(212) 808-6600
(212) 808-6898 (fax)

45. *The Washington Post*
1150 15th Street NW
Washington, DC 20071
(202) 334-6000
(202) 334-5693 (fax)

46. *The Washington Times*
3600 New York Ave. NW.
Washington, DC 20002
(202) 636- 3000

News Magazines

1. *Newsweek*
251 W. 57th Street
New York, NY 10019
(212) 445-4000
(212) 445-5068 (fax)

2. *Time*
Time and Life Building
Rockefeller Center
1271 Avenue of Americas
New York, NY 10020
(212) 522-1212
(212) 765-2699 (fax)

3. *U. S. News & World Report*
2400 N Street, NW
Washington, DC 20037
(202) 955-2000
(2020 955-2049 (fax)

Appendix H

Selected List of Muslim Media: Newspapers, Magazines, Periodicals, Audio-video and Software Producers, Radio, and Television Programs

1. *Aljumuah* (Monthly / English)
   P. O. Box 5387
   Madison, WI 53705-5387
   608-277-1855

2. *Al-Nashra*, The Arab American Magazine (Monthly/ English)
   Arab Media House
   P. O. Box 248
   Arlington, VA 22210
   703-271-8538

3. *Al-Zaitonah* (Monthly/Arabic)
   P. O. Box 742342
   Dallas, TX 75374-2342

4. *American Journal of Islamic Finance* (Bi-monthly / English)
   27957 Ridgebluff CT.
   Rancho Palos Verdas, CA 90274
   310-544-9618

5. *American Journal of Islamic Social Sciences* (Quarterly/ English)
   555 Grove Street
   P.O.Box 669
   Herndon, VA 22070
   703-471-1133

6. The Voice of Islam Radio
   515 Madison Ave,. # 1303
   New York, NY 10022
   516-889-0005

7. *Assirat Al-Mustaqeem* (Monthly / Arabic)
P. O. Box 71314
Pittsburgh PA 15213
412-531-9566

8. Astrolabe Pictures (Children Video)
585 Grove Street, Suite 300
Herndon, VA 20170
800-392-7876

9. Digitek (Islamic Software)
7631 Leesburg Pike, Suite B
Falls Church, VA 22043
800-333-SAKHR
www.sakhr.com

10. Discover Islam Poster Exhibits
Transcom International Inc.
7360 McWhorter Place, Suite 201
Annandale, VA 22003
703-941-7783

11. Home Interactive (Interactive Arabic/English CD ROM)
1250 E. walnut, Suite 136
Pasadena, CA 91106
800-381-1242

12. *IQRA* (English)
325 North Third Street
San Jose, CA 95112
408-947-9389

13. ISL Software Corp (Computer software)
2037 Featherwood Street
Silver Spring, MD 20904-6645
800-443-3636

14. *Islamic Horizon* (Bi-monthly / English)
P. O. Box 38
Plainfield, IN 46168
317-839-8157

15. Islamic Information Service ((TV/Radio Program Producers)
7336 Hinds Ave.
Los Angeles, CA 9105
818-764-6611

16. *Journal of Islamic Medical Association* (Quarterly/English)
818 St. Sebastian Way, Suite 200
Augusta, GA 30901

17. Lighthouse Media (Television Program Producers)
P. O. Box 51123
Indianapolis, IN 46251
317-240-1999

18. Micro Systems International (Quran CD ROM)
505 S. Neil Street
Champaign, IL 61820
217-356-7226

19. *Muslim Journal* (Weekly / English)
910 W. Van Buren, Suite 100
Chicago, IL 60607
312-243-7600

20. *Muslim World Monitor* (Monthly / English)
P. O. Box 741805
Dallas, TX 75374
214-669-9595

21. *New Trend* (Bi-weekly / English)
P. O. Box 356
Kingsville, MD 21087

22. *Pakistan Link* (Bi-weekly / English))
P. O. Box 351447
Carson, CA 90745
310-513-6397

23. SAKKAL Design (Computer Graphic Des. software)
1523 175 Place SE
Bothell, WA 98012
206-483-8830

24. Sound Vision (Video/Multimedia)
1327 W. Washington Blvd., # 105
Chicago, IL 60607
800-432-4262; 312-226-0205
info@soundvision.com; www.soundvision.com

25. *The Message* (Monthly / English)
166-26 89th Ave.
Jamaica, NY 11432
718-658-5163

26. *The Minaret* (Monthly /English)
434 S. Vermont Ave.
Los Angeles, CA 90020
213-384-4570

27. *The Minaret Newspaper* (Thrice a month/ English)
1133 Broadway, Suite 539
New York, NY 10010
212-989-2831

28. *Washington Report on Middle East Affairs*
(Monthly / English))
P. O. Box 53062
Washington, D. C. 20009
202-939-6050

29. *Young Muslim* (Monthly / English)
1327 W. Washington Blvd., # 105
Chicago, IL 60607
800-432-4262
youngmuslim@soundvision.com

Appendex I

A Selected List of Muslim Financial Organizations

1. AMANA Mutual Fund (Investment)
1300 N. State Street
Bellingham, WA 98227
800-728-1266

2. American Finance House LARIBA (Interest Free Loans/Investment)
750 E. Green Street, Suite 210
Pasadena, CA 91101
818-449-4401

3. BMI Finance & Investment (Interest Free Loans/ Investment)
One Harmon Plaza
Secaucus, NJ 07094
201-865-8096

4. First Path Financial Services (Financial Services)
27957 Ridgebluff CT.
Rancho Palos Verdas, CA 90274
310-544-9618

5. Islamic Housing Cooperative Corporation (Interst Free Loans)
11441 Ladue Road
St. Louis, MO 63141
314-291-3711

6. MSI Finance Corporation (Interesr Free Loans / Investment)
9801 Westheimer, Suite 302
Houston, TX 77042
800-USA-MSI1

7. Muslim Community Credit Union (Financial Services)
5070 Parkside Ave.
Philadelphia, PA 19131
215-879-8500

8. Muslim United Economic Development (Financial Counselling / Services)
   207 Florida Ave. NW
   Washington, D. C. 20004
   202-667-2950

9. Samad Group (Investment / Finacial Services)
   2801 Far Hills Ave., Suite 20
   Dayton, OH 45419
   513-436-3624

10. SANA Financial Inc. (Leasing Finance)
    375 W. 63rd Street
    Burridge, IL 60521
    630-789-8593

Appendix J

Major Muslim Organizations in the U. S.

1. Federation of Islamic Associations (FIA)
   25341 Five Mile Road
   Redford Twp., MI 48239
   313-534-3295

2. Islamic Assembly of North America (IANA)
   3588 Plymouth Road, #270
   Ann Arbor, MI 48105
   313-528-0006
   IANA@IANAnet.ORG

3. Islamic Circle of North America (ICNA)
   166-26 89th Avenue
   Jamaica, NY 11432
   718-658-1199
   ICNA@aol.com

4. Islamic Shura Council
   c/o: ICNA; see above

5. Islamic Society of North America (ISNA)
   P. O. Box 38
   Plainfield, IN 46168
   317-839-8157
   isna@surf-ici.com

6. Ministry of Imam W. Deen Mohammed
   266 Madison
   Calumet City, Il 60409
   708-862-5228

7. Muslim Arab Youth Association (MAYA)
   2485 Directors Row, Suite E
   Indianapolis, IN 46241
   317-247-0844

8. Muslim Students Association of U. S. & Canada (MSA)
   P. O. Box 38
   Plainfield, IN 46168
   317-839-8157

9. The Council of Masajids of U.S.A. Inc.
   134 W. 26th Street, 11th floor
   New York, NY 10001
   21-627-4033

10. The National Community
    1128 Oak Street
    Atlanta, GA 30310
    404-758-7016

Appendix K

Muslim Professional Associations, Research Institutes, and Political Organizations
A Selected List

1. American Muslim Council (Political/ lobbying)
   1212 New York Ave, Suite 525
   Washington, D. C. 20005
   202-789-2262

2. Association of Muslim Scientists & Engineers (Professional)
   P. O. Box 38
   Plainfield, IN 46168
   317-593-5028

3. Association of Muslim Social Scientists (Professional)
   555 Grove Street
   Herndon, VA 22070
   703-471-1133

4. Center for American Muslim Research & Information (Research)
   103-43 Lefferts Blvd.
   Richmond Hill, NY 11419
   718-848-8952

5. Council of American Islamic Relations (Media monitoring/ relations)
   1511 K Street, N. W., Suite 807
   Washington, D. C. 20005
   202-638-6340

6. International Institute of Islamic Thought (Research)
   555 Grove Street
   Herndon, VA 22070
   703-471-1133

7. Islamic Medical Association (Professional)
950 75th Street
Downers Grove, IL 60516
630-852-2122

8. Muslim American Bar Association (Professional)
1212 New York Ave., Suite 525
Washington, D. C. 20005
202-789-2262

9. Muslim Public Affairs Council (Political/lobbying)
3010 Wilshire Blvd., Suite 217
Los Angeles, CA 90010
213-383-3443

10. North American Association of Muslim Professionals & Scholars (Professional)
P. O. Box 6083
Macomb, IL 61455
309-298-1326

Appendix L

Muslim Service Organizations, Bookstores, and Publishers A Selected List

1. Al-Meezan International (Children's Islamic Book Publisher)
   125 Vincent Drive
   Bolingbrook, Il 60440
   630-759-4981

2. Alminar (Bookseller)
   450 Atlantic Avenue
   Brooklyn, NY 11217
   718-875-5366

3. AMANA Corporation (Publisher)
   4411 41st Street
   Brentwood, MD 20722
   301-779-7774

4. American Islamic College (Higher-Educational Institution)
   640 W. Irving Park Road
   Chicago, IL 60613
   773-281-4700

5. American Trust Publications (Publishers)
   10900 W. Washungton Street
   Indianapolis, IN 46231
   317-839-9278

6. Bosnia Relief Fund, Inc. (Relief for Bosnian Muslims)
   P.O.Box 91825
   1024 Fairview Drive
   Elk Grove, IL 60009
   847-616-8223

7. Council on Islamic Education (Resource and Research on Public Education)
   P. O. Box 20186
   9300 Gardenia Street, #B-3
   Fountain Valley, CA 92728-0186
   714-839-2929

8. East-West University (Higher-Educational Institution)
   816 S. Michigan Ave.
   Chicago, Il 60605
   312-939-0111

9. Edhi Foundation (Pakistan-based Relief Organization)
   42-07 National Street
   Corona, NY 11368
   718-639-5120

10. Halalco Books (Booksellers)
    108 E. Fairfax Street
    Falls Church, VA 22046
    703-532-3202

11. Holy Land Foundation (Relief Organization for Palestine)
    P. O. Box 832390
    1710 Ferman Drive, Suite 100
    Richardsson, TX 75083
    214-699-9868

12. IQRA International Educational Foundations (Educational Research/ Publishers & Booksellers)
    7450 Skokie Blvd.
    Skokie, IL 60077
    847-673-4072
    800-521-4272 (Mail order)

13. ICNA Book Service (Book Sellers)
    166-26 89th Ave.
    Jamaica, NY 11432
    718-657-4090

14. Indian Muslim Relief Committee (Relief Organization for Muslims in India)
800 San Antonio Road, Suite 1
Palo Alto, CA 94303
415-856-0440

15. Institute of Islamic Information & Education (Dawah & Islamic Information)
4390 N. Elston Ave.
Chicago, IL 60641
773-777-7443

16. International Relief Organization (Relief)
1612 D Street, NW, Suite 1200
Washington, D. C. 20006
202-223-4262

17. Islamic Book Service (Bookseller)
10900 W. Washungton Street
Indianapolis, IN 46231
317-839-9278

18. Islamic Books & Tapes Supply
P. O. Box 5153
Long Island City, NY 11105
718-721-4246
800-337-4287

19. Islamic Correctional Union Reunion Association (Dawah in Prison)
P. O. Box 774
6336 S. 66th Ave.
Tinley Park, IL 60477
708-429-0093

20. Kazi Publications (Publishers/ Booksellers)
3023 W. Belmont Ave.
Chicago, IL 60618
773-267-7001

21. Mercy International (Relief)
P. O. Box 248
31967 Block street
Garden City, MI 48136
313-421-2273

22. Multimedia Vera International (Publisher/
Bookseller/Video/audio)
434 S. Vermont
Los Angeles, CA 90020
213-381-5762

23. NAAMPS Publications (Publishers)
640 W. Irving Park Road
Chicago, IL 60613
773-281-4700

Appendix M

Islamic Centers and Mosques in areas of significant Muslim population*

Alabama

1.Birmingham Islamic Society
1128 S. 14th St.
Birmingham, AL 35205
205-933-2913

2. Masjid Al-Quran
3424 26th Street North
Birmingham, AL 35207
205-324-0212

3. Tulsacola Islamic Center
728 22nd Ave.
Tulsacola, AL 35401
205-556-0685`

4. Tuskgee Masjid
1508 Adam Street
Tuskgee, AL 36088
205-727-8011

5. Islamic Society of Mobile
63 E. drive
Mobile, AL 36608
205-343-4695

6. Muslim Community Association of Auburn & Opelika
338 Armstrong Street
Auburn, AL 36830
205-821-8307

* Estimate of the total number of Islamic centers and mosques in the U. S. vary from one source to another. For example, Koszegi (1992) in his book, *Islam in North America*, has listed about 1300 centers and mosques in the U. S., Islamic Resource Institute's Directory (1994) lists about 1000 centers and mosques, and the Resource Directory of Islam in America (1994) accounts for about 1900 centers and mosques. It is estimated that there are more than 2000 Islamic Centers and mosques in the U. S. at present. This appendix provides a selective list of Islamic Centers in areas of significant Muslim population: A center or mosque where the average Friday Prayer attendance is 50 or more. Due care is taken in preparing this list, still it is possible that some major centers' name may have been left unintentionally.

Alaska

7. Islamic Center of Alaska
4141 Ingra, #202
Anchorage, AK 99503
907-562-4241

Arizona

8. Islamic Community Center
5301 N. 30th Drive
Phoenix, AZ 85041
602-268-6151

9. Islamic Center of Tucson
901 E. 1st St.
Tucson, AZ 85719
602-624-3233

10. Masjid Ibrahim
2075 Airway Ave.
Kingman, AZ 86401
602-757-8822/2367

Arkansas

11. Masjid Amin Zakariyyah
1717 Wright Ave.
Little Rock, AR 72203
501-372-1942

California

12. Masjid Umar Ibn
Al Khattab
1025 Exposition Blvd.
Los Angeles, CA 90007
213-733-9938

13. Masjid Felix Bilal
4016 S. Central Ave.
Los Angeles, CA 90011
213-233-7274

14. Islamic Center of Southern California
434 S. Vermont Ave.
Los Angeles, CA 90020
213-382-9200

15. Masjid As Salam
2900 W. Florence
Los Angeles, CA 90043
213-758-4033

16. Masjid Bilal Ibn Rabah
5450 Crenshaw Blvd.
Los Angeles, CA 90043
213-755-3807

17. Islamic Society of West Los Angeles
4117 Overland Ave.
Culver City, CA 90232
213-837-5512

18. Husseini Mosque
7925 Serapis St.
P. O. Box 34309
Pico Rivera, CA 90660
310-926-1914

19. Islamic Center of South Bay
25816 Walnut Street
Lomita, CA 90717
310-534-1363

20. Masjid Al-Taqwa
2551 N. Fair Oaks Ave.
Pasadena, CA 91001
818-398-8392

21. Islamic Center of St. Gabriel Valley
19164 E. Walnut Drive North
Rowland Hts., CA 91748
818-964-3596

22. Islamic Center of San Diego
7050 Eckstrom Ave.
San Diego, CA 92111
619-278-5240

23. Islamic Society of Orange County
9752 W. 13th Street
Garden Grove, CA 92642
714-531-1722

24. Islamic Center of San Francisco
400 Crescent Ave.
San Francisco, CA 94110
415-282-9039

25. San Francisco Muslim Community Center
850 Divisadero St.
San Francisco, CA 94117
415-563-9397

26. Fremont Islamic Center
3535 Capitol Ave.
Fremont, CA 94538
510-795-7137

27. Masjid Al Islam
8210 MacArthur Blvd.
Oakland, CA 94605
415-638-9541

28. Islamic Center of Berkeley
2510 Channing way
Berkeley, CA 94704
415-549-9465

29. Masjid Al-Noor
1755 Catherine St.
Santa Clara, CA 95050
408-246-9822

30. Islamic Center of San Jose
325 N. 3rd St.
San Jose, CA 95112
408-947-9389

31. Islamic Center
539 Russel Blvd.
Davis, CA 95616
916-756-5216

32. Islamic Center of Woodland
1023 North Street
Woodland, CA 95695
916-666-4706

33. Islamic Center of Sacramento
2011 4th Street
Sacramento, CA 95818
916-444-6323

34. Islamic Center
3600 Tiera Buena
Yuba City, CA 95993
916-674-5334

Colorado

35. Masjid Al-Nur
2124 S. Birch Street
Denver, CO 80224
303-759-1985

36. Colorado Muslim Society
2071 S. Parker Street
Denver, CO 80204
303-696-9800

37. Islamic Center of Boulder
1530 Culver CT.
Boulder, CO 80303
303-444-6345

38. Islamic Society of Colorado Springs
4820 Rusina Road, Suite C
Colorado Springs, CO 80907
719-528-5463

Connecticut

39. Madina Masjid
1 Madina Drive
Windsor, CT 06095
203-249-0112

40. Masjid Muhammad
64 Carmel Street
New Haven, CT 06511
203-562-0594

41. New Heaven Islamic Center
2 Pruden Street
West Heaven, CT 06516
203-933-5799

42. Bridgeport Islamic Society
1300 Fairfield
Bridgeport, CT 06601
203-579-2211

43. Albanian American Muslim Community
38 Raymond Street
Waterbury, CT 06706
203-879-3680

Delaware

44. Islamic Society of Delaware
28 Salem Church Road
Newark, DE 19713
203-733-0373

45. The Muslim Center of Wilmington
301 W. 6th Street
Wilmington, DE 19801
302-571-0532

District of Columbia

46. Masjid Muhammad
1519 Islamic Way (4th St.) N.W.
Washington, D. C. 20002
202-483-8832

47. Islamic Center of Washington D. C.
2551 Massachusetts Ave., N. W.
Washington, D. C. 20008
202-332-8343

Florida

48. Daytona Beach Masjid
347 S. Keach Street
Daytona Beach, FL 32114
904-252-3501

49. Islamic Center of Northeast Florida
2333 S. St. john Bluff Road
Jacksonville, FL 32209
904-646-3462

50. Masjid Al-Ansar
1020 W. Pensacola St.
Tallahassee. FL 32401
904-681-9022

51. Islamic Center
1010 W. University Ave.
Gainsville, FL 32601
904-372-7980

52. Islamic Society of Central Florida
1005 N. Goldenrod Road
Orlando, FL 32816
407-273-8363

53. Islamic Center of Orlando
11543 Ruby Lake Road
Orlando, FL 32836
407-238-0266

54. Miami Masjid
7350 N. W. 3rd St.
Miami, FL 33126
305-261-7622

55. Masjid Markaz Al Islam
4305 N. W. 183rd St.
Miami, FL 33169
305-624-5555

56. Masjid Tawhid
1557 N. W. 5th Street
Ft. Lauderdale, Fl 33311
305-581-6295

57. Islamic Society of Tempa Bay Area
7326 E. Sligh Ave.
Tampa, FL 33610
813-628-9081

58. Islamic Center of W. Florida
3337 Broadway
Fort Myers, FL 33902
813-939-0292

Georgia

59. Islamic Center of Imam Jamil Al-Amin
1126 Oak Street
Atlanta, GA 30310
404-758-7016

60. Masjid of Islam
560 Fayetteville Road S. E.
Atlanta, GA 30316
404-378-1600

61. Al-Huda Islamic Center
2022 S. Milledge Ave.
Athens, GA 30605
706-548-4620

62. Islamic Center of Augusta
1005 N. Goldenrod Road
Augusta, GA 30907
706-868-7278

Hawaii

63. Islamic Center
1395 Aleo Place
Honolulu, HI 96822
808-947-6263

Idaho

64. Islamic Center of Boise
4911 Morris Hills
Boise, ID 83725
208-342-2033

65. Masjid Omar
316 Lilley, P. O. Box 4025
Moscow, ID 83843
208-882-8312

Illinois

66. Islamic Society of northwest Suburbs
3890 Industrial Drive
Rolling Meadows, Il 60008
847-253-6400

67. Islamic Association of Des Plaines
480 Potter road
Des Plaines, IL 60016
847-824-1100

68. Islamic Cultural Center
1810 N. Pfingston Road
Northbrook, IL 60062
847-272-0319

69. Islamic Community Center
345 Heine Ave.
Elgin, IL 60123
847-695-3338

70. Albanian American Islamic Center
5825 S. St. Charles Road
Berkeley, IL 60163
708-544-2609

71. Islamic Foundation
300 W. Highridge Road
Villa Park, IL 60181
630-941-0511

72. Masjid Al-Islam
560 E. Frontage Road
Bolingbrook, IL 60440
630-972-0701

73. Mosque Foundation of Chicago
7360 W. 93rd. Street
Bridgeview, IL 60455
708-430-5666

74. Downtown Islamic Center
218 S. Wabash Street, 5th floor
Chicago, IL 60603
312-939-9095

75. American Islamic College Mosque
640 W. Irving Park Road
Chicago, IL 60613
773-281-4700

76. Nigerian Islamic Association
932 W. Sheridan Road
Chicago, IL 60613

77. Muslim Community Center
4380 N. Elston Ave.
Chicago, IL 60641

78. Masjid Al-Fatir
1200 E. 47th Street
Chicago, IL 60653
773-268-7248

79. Muslim Association of Greater Rockford
5921 Darlene Drive
Rockford, IL 61109
815-397-3311

80. Islamic Center of Quad-Cities
3061 7th Street
Moline, IL 61265
309-762-0768

81. Islamic Center of Greater Peoria
Spring Creek & Cruger Road
Washington, IL 61571
309-745-8410

82. Islamic Center
106 S. Lincoln
Urbana, IL 61801
217-344-0022

83. Islamic Society of Greater Springfield
P. O. Box 92
Springfield, IL 62705
217-787-5636

84. Islamic Center
511 S. Popular
Carbondale, IL 62901
618-457-2770

Indiana

85. Masjid Al-Fajr
2846 Cold Spring Road
Indianapolis, IN 46222
317-923-2847

86. Islamic Center
P.O.Box 51623
Indianapolis, IN 46251
317-839-8157

87. Islamic Center
P.O.Box 710, Brown Road
Michigan City, IN 46360
219-233-3513

88. Masjid Al-Amin
3702 W. 11th Ave.
Gary, IN 46404
219-949-1854

89. Gary Masjid
1473 W. 15th Ave.
Gary, IN 46407
219-885-3010

90. Islamic Center
809 E. 8th Street
Bloomington, IN 47401
812-333-1611

91. Islamic Center
1319 6th Street
Terre Haute, IN 47802
812-237-7562

Iowa

92. Islamic Center of Des Moines
6201 Franklin Ave.
Des Moines, IA 50322
515-255-0212

93. Islamic Center
114 E. Prentiss Street
Iowa City, IA 52244
319-354-6167

94. Islamic Center and Mosque
2999 First Ave. S. W.
Cedar Rapids, IA 52405
319-362-0857

95. Mother Mosque
1335 9th St., N. W.
Cedar Rapids, IA 52405
319-366-3150

Kansas

96. Islamic Center
1300 Ohio Street
Lawrence. KS 66044
913-749-1638

97. Islamic Center
1224 Hylton Heights
Manhattan, KS 66502
913-776-8543

98. Masjid Al-Noor
3104 E. 17th Street
Wichita, KS 67208
316-687-4936

Kentucky

99. Faisal Mosque
4007 N. Upper River Road
Louisville, KY 40207
502-893-9466

100. Islamic Center
1715 S. 4th Street
Louisville, KY 40508
502-624-1395

101. Islamic Cutural Association of Louisville
1911 Buchell Bank Road
Louisville, KY 40220
502-491-2979

102. Islamic Center
649 S. Limestone Street
Lexington, KY 40508
606-255-0335

Louisiana

103. New Orleans Islamic Center
1911 St. Claude Ave.
New Orleans, LA 70116
504-94-3758

104. Masjid Al-Ghurba
6244 Waldo Drive
New Orleans, LA 70148
504-282-0700

105. Islamic Center
820 W. Chimes
Baton Rouge, LA 70802
504-387-3617

Maryland

106. Muslim Community Center
15200 New Hampshire Ave.
Silver Spring, MD 20905
301-384-3454

107. Masjid Ar Rahmah
6631 Johnycake Road
Baltimore, MD 21207
410-747-4869

108. Masjidul Haqq
514 Islamic Way (Wilson)
Baltimore, MD 21218
410-728-1363

Massachusetts

109. Masjid Ibn Al-arqam
57 Laurel Street
Worchester, MA 01604
508-752-4377

110. Islamic Center of Boston
126 Boston Post Road
Wayland, MA 01778
508-358-5885

111. Islamic Center of New England
470 South Street
Quincy, MA 02169
617-479-8341

Michigan

112. Islamic Center
2301 Plymouth Road
Ann Arbor, MI 48105
313-665-8882

113. American Muslim Society
9945 W. Vernor Highway
Dearborn, MI 48126
313-846-3498

114. Islamic Center of Detroit
4646 Cass Ave.
Detroit, MI 48201
313-831-9222

115. Masjid Wali Muhammad
11529 Hon. Elijah Muhammad Blvd.
Detroit, MI 48206
313-893-7951

116. Islamic Mosque of America
16427 W. Warren Ave.
Detroit, MI 48228
313-582-0500

117. Islamic Association of Greater Detroit
879 W. Auburn
Rochester, MI 48307
313-852-5657

118. Flint Masjid of Islam
402 E. Glispie
Flint, MI 48532
313-767-6591

119. Islamic Center
920 S. Harrison Road
E. Lansing, MI 48823
517-351-4309

120 Klamazoo Islamic Center
1520 W. Michigan Ave.
Kalamazoo, MI 49005
606-381-6611

121. Islamic Center
1301 Burton Ave. S. E.
Grand Rapids, MI 49505
616-241-4555

Minnesota

122. Islamic Center of Minneapolis
1128 6th Street SE
Minneapolis, MN 55414
612-571-5604

123. Masjid An-Nur
1810 Bryant Ave. N
Minneapolis, MN 55411
612-521-0245

Mississippi

124. Masjid Umar Bin Khattab
2533 Old McDowell Road
Jackson, MS 39284
601-371-2834

125. Biloxi Islamic Center
205 Keller Ave.
Biloxi, MS 39530
601-432-7650

Missouri

126. Islamic Center of Greater St. Louis
3843 W. Pine Street
St. Louis, MO 63108
314-534-9672

127. Islamic Soc. of Greater Kansas City
8501 E. 99th Street
Kansas City, MO 64134
816-763-2267

128. Islamic Center
1201 S. 5th Street
Columbia, MO 65204
314-875-4633

Montana

129. Islamic Center
P. O.Box 121
Billings, MT 59103
406-245-4551

Nebraska

130. Islamic Center
3511 N. 73rd Street
Omaha, NE 68104
402-571-0720

131. Islamic Foundation
3636 N. First Street
Lincoln, NE 68501
402-475-0475

Nevada

132. Islamic Society of Nevada
4730 E. Desert Inn Road
Las Vegas, NV 89121
702-433-3431

133. Islamic Center of Reno
1295 Valley Road
Reno, NV 89512
702-786-2522

New Hampshire

134. Islamic Society
230 Main Street
SALEM, NH 03079
603-893-1112

New Jersey

135. Islamic Cultural Center
420-24 Bradford Pl.
Newark, NJ 07101
201-623-2991

136. Turkish Mosque of America
103 Elmwood Ave.
Newark, NJ 07104
201-482-8996

137. Islamic Center of Newark
210-216 Clinton Pl.
Newark, NJ 07112
201-824-3764

138. Islamic Center of Jersey City
17 Park Street
Jersey City, NJ 07304
201-433-0057

139. Masjid As-Salaam
984 West Side Ave.
Jersey City, NJ 07306
201-332-9588

140. Islamic Center of Passaic /Patterson
245 Broadway
Patterson, NJ 07501
201-279-4151

141. Masjid Muhammad
107 I. S. Cole Plaza
Atlantic City, NJ 08401
609-347-0788

142. Islamic Society of Central Jersey
US 1 South & Stouts Lane
Monmouth Jumction, NJ 08852
908-329-8126

New Mexico

143 Islamic Center of New Mexico
1100 Yale Blvd., SE
Albuquerque, NM 87106
505-256-1450

144. Dar Al-Islam
P.O.Box 146
Abiquiu, NM 87510
505-685-4515

New York

145. Madina Masjid
401 E. 11th Street
New York, NY 10009
212-533-5060

146. Masjid Malcolm Shabazz
102 West 116th St.
New York, NY 10026
212-662-2200

147. Masjid An-Noor
104 Rhine Ave.
Staten Island, NY 10314
718-442-6674

148. Masjid Taqwa
901 Anderson Ave.
Bronx, NY 10453
212- 731-2800

149. Islamic Center of Astoria
21-23 30th Drive
Astoria, NY 11102
718-728-2601

150. Masjid Ikhwa
1135 Eastern Parkway
Brooklyn, NY 11216
718-493-0461

151. Masjid Al Taqwa
1266 Bedford Ave.
Brooklyn, NY 11216
718-622-0800

152. Bangladesh Muslim Center
1013 Church Ave.
Brooklyn, NY 11218
718-282-9230

153. Makki Masjid
1089 Coney Island Ave.
Brooklyn, NY 11230
718-859-4485

154. Muslim Center of New York
137-63 Kalmia Ave.
Flushing, NY 11355
718-445-2642

155. Al-Markaz
166-26 89th Ave.
Jamaica, NY 11432
718-658-1199

156 Islamic Center of Long Island
835 Brush Hollow Road
Westbury, NY 11590
516-333-3495

157. Muslim Center
P. O. Box 907
Albany, NY 12210
518-449-8578

158. Islamic Society of Central New York
925 Comstock Ave.
Syracuse, NY 13210
315-637-3945

159. Islamic Society of Niagara Frontier
40 Parker Street
Buffalo, NY 14214
716-836-9789

160. Islamic Center of Rochester
62 Farmingham Lane
Rochester, NY 14692
716-442-0117

161. Ithaca Muslim Community
Cornell 218 Anable Taylor Hall
Ithaca, NY 14853
607-277-6706

North Carolina

162. Community Mosque of Winston-Salem
1326 E. 3rd Street
Winston-Salem, NC 27101
919-724-5554

163. Islamic Society of Greensboro
2109 Martin Luther King Drive
Greensboro, NC 27420
919-379-7445

164. Islamic Center of Raleigh
3020 Ligon Street
Raleigh, NC 27607
919-834-9572

165. Islamic Center of Charlotte
1700 Progress Street
Charlotte, NC 28229
704-532-9008

166. Masjid Mustafa
P. O. Box 35063
Charlotte, NC 28235
704-841-8298

North Dakota

167. Islamic Society of Fargo-Moorehead
P.O.Box 5223
Fargo, ND 58105
701-234-9607

Ohio

168. Masjid Al-Islam
1677 Oak Street
Columbus, OH 43203
614-252-0338

169. Islamic Foundation of Central Ohio
1428 E. Broad Street
Columbus, OH 43551
614-253-3251

170. Islamic Center of Greater Toledo
25877 Schrieder Road
Perrysburg, OH 43551
419-874-3509

171. Islamic Center
724 Techumseh Street
Toledo, OH 43602
419-241-9522

172. Islamic Center of Greater Cleveland
9400 Detroit Ave.
Cleveland, OH 44102
216-281-6007

173. Masjid Warith Deen
7301 Superior Ave.
Cleveland, OH 44108

174. First Cleveland Mosque
3613 E. 131 Street
Cleveland, OH 44120
216-283-9027

175. Islamic Society of Greater Akron
668 Summer
Akron, OH 44311
216-535-3666

176. Cincinnati Islamic Center
3809 Woodford Road
Cincinnati, OH 45213
513-793-4508

177. Islamic Center of Dayton
26 Josie Street
Dayton, OH 45403
513-277-1805

Oklahoma

178. Masjid Al-Islam
525 N. University Drive
Edmond, OK 73034
405-741-1077

179. Masjid An Nur
420 E. Lindsey Street
Normon, OK 73069
405-364-5747

180. Masjid Al-Muminun
1322 N.E. 23rd Street
Oklahoma City, OK 73111
405-424-1471

181. Al Siddiq Mosque
616 N. Washington
Stillwater, OK 74075
405-377-5910

182. Islamic Community Center
1436 N. Chyeene
Tulsa, OK 74106
918-587-1132

Oregon

183. Muslim Community Center
3801 NE Martin Luther King Blvd
Portland, OR 97207
503-281-7691

184. Abubakar Siddiq Islamic Center
1856 W. Broadway
Eugene, OR 97402
503-485-0899

Pennsylvania

185. Islamic Center (Masjid Daressalaam)
P.O.Box 19763
Pittsburgh, PA 15208
412-682-5555

186. Masjid Al-Awwal (First Muslim Mosque)
1911 Wylie Ave.
Pittsburgh, PA 15219
412-471-1036

187. Islamic Soc. of Central Pennsylvania
10185 Calder Square
State College, PA 17103
814-238-2079

188. Islmic Center
1725 Martin Luther King Blvd
Harrisburg, PA 17104
717-232-4545

189. Masjid Baba Muhayaddeen
5820 Overbrook Ave.
Philadelphia, PA 19131
215-879-6300

190. Philadelphia Masjid
4700 Wyalusing Ave.
Philadelphia, PA 19131
215-877-8600

191. Makkah Masjid
1319 W. Susquehanna Ave.
Philadelphia, PA 19132
215-978-9508

Rhode Island

192. Masjid Al Karim
580 Cranston Street
Providence, RI 02907
401-274-3986

South Carolina

193. Masjid Assalaam
5119 Monticello Road
Columbia, SC 29203
803-252-9477

194. Madinah Masjid
195 Line Street
Charleston, SC 2229403

South Dakota

195. Islamic Society of Brookings
803 13th Ave.
Brookings, SD 57006

Tennessee

196. Islamic Center of Nashville
2515 12th Ave. South
Nashville, TN 37204
615-385-9379

197. The Islamic Center
1410 Cemetery Ave.
Chattanooga, TN 37408
615-756-4917

198. Muslim Community-Knoxville
100 13th Street
Knoxville, TN 37916
615-637-8172

199.Muslim Society of Memphis
1065 Stratford
Memphis, TN 38122
901-685-8906

Texas

200. Dallas Masjid of Al-Islam
2604 S. Harwood Street
Dallas, TX 75215
214-421-3839

201. Islamic Society of Arlington
100 Madinah Road
Arlington, TX 76010
817-461-8415

202. Masjid Al-Jamia
4801 Fletcher Ave.
Fortworth, TX 76107
817-737-8104

203. Islamic Society of Greater Houston
12222 Cedargap
Houston, TX 40601
713-667-6525

204. ISGH Southeast Zone
8830 Old Galvaston Road
Houston, TX 77034
713-947-0394

205. ISGH Northwest Zone
1209 Conard Sauer Dr.
Houston, TX 77043
713-464-4720

206. ISGH North Zone
11815 Adel Road
Houston, TX 77067
713-537-1946

207. Masjid Al-Isra
4105 Garden Dale
San Antonio, TX 78229
210-614-0989

208. Austin Mosque
1906 Neuces Street
Austin, TX 78705
512-495-9590

209. Islamic Center
1600 N. Kansas
El Paso, TX 79902
919-546-9468

Utah

210. Islamic Soc. of Salt Lake City
740 S. 700 East
Salt Lake City, UT 84102
801-364-7822

Virginia

211. Dar Al-Hijra
3159 Row Street
Falls Church, VA 22044
703-536-1030

212. Islamic Center of Virginia
1241 Buford Road
Richmond, VA 23235
804-320-7333

213. Norfolk Masjid
3401 Granby Street
Norfolk, VA 23504
804-423-2305

<u>Washington</u>

214. Islamic Center
1420 NE Northgate Way
Seattle, WA 98125
206-363-3013

215. Islamic Center
2010 Bridgeport Way
Tacoma, WA 98466
206-459-1993

216. Masjid Al Farooq
NE 1155 Stadium Way
Pullman, WA 99163
509-334-9424

217.Spokane Islamic Center
E. 505 Wedgewood
Spokane, WA 99208
509-482-2608

<u>West Virginia</u>

218. Muslim Ass. of Huntington
1628 13th Ave.
Huntington, WV 25701
304-291-6720

<u>Wisconsin</u>

219. Masjid Tawheed
6001 88th Ave.
Kenosha, WI 53140
414-654-0575

220. Islamic Center
4707 S. 13th Street
Milwaukee, WI 53221
414-282-1812

221. MSA of U of Wisconsin
21 N. Orchard Street
Madison, WI 53715
608-251-4668

Wyoming

222. Islamic Center of Larmie
577 N. 11th Street
Larmie, WY 82070
307-721-3065

Index